GRAND LARCENIES

Translations and Imitations of Ten Dutch Poets

GRAND LARCENIES

Translations and Imitations of Ten Dutch Poets

translated and edited by P.C. Evans

CARCANET POETRY

First published in Great Britain in 2021 by
Carcanet
Alliance House, 30 Cross Street
Manchester, M2 7AQ
www.carcanet.co.uk

A CIP catalogue record for this book is
available from the British Library.

ISBN 978 1 80017 132 9

Book design by Andrew Latimer
Printed in Great Britain by SRP Ltd, Exeter, Devon

This book was published with the support of the Dutch Foundation for
Literature.

The publisher acknowledges financial
assistance from Arts Council England.

CONTENTS

J. EIJKELBOOM

H. H. TER BALKT

K. MICHEL

ESTHER JANSMA

INTRODUCTION

The first recorded lines of poetry written in Dutch – or Old Flemish – are from the late 11th century: *Hebban olla vogala nestas hagunnan hinase hic enda thu wat unbidan we nu. (Do all of the birds have nests, but for you and me; well, what are we waiting for).* They were composed in the Benedictine abbey of St Andrew's in Rochester, and only discovered in the Bodleian in 1933 on a flyleaf of a manuscript of Anglo-Saxon sermons. The lines are a pen test and they appear beneath the Latin version *Abent omnes volucres nidos inceptos nisi ego et tu quid expectamus nunc.* So, which came first? Given the internal rhyme and double entendre of the Dutch, and the woodenness of the Latin, my vote would go to the demotic. This is the Netherlands' *Sumer is icumen in.*

The poet in question was likely to have been a Flemish monk, seconded from the Norman abbey of *Notre Dame du Bec Hellouin,* a pan-European publishing powerhouse, and centre for the training of scribes. England had recently been annexed by the Normans and our poet would have been a servant of the new European Raj. But, was our scribe merely regurgitating an extant verse by another hand? Or was this an original composition? And what might his motivation have been for doodling the poem on the sermons? Was this perhaps Auden's bored clerk? Or was he, as I suspect, more in thrall to Eros? And what could the circumstances of this poem's composition possibly tell us about modern Dutch poetry?

By and large, the Dutch are pretty a-historical. There's little kowtowing to the past, apart from the odd twinge of the phantom limb of the 17th century Golden Age. Literary-wise, you won't get much of a nod and a wink these days to anything before the revolutionary neo-Impressionist movement of the 1880s with its *L'art pour l'art*, and 'orgies / full of music and unspeakable joy'. Here, the spirit of Shelley looms large. The movement was a reaction against the so-called 'preacher-poets' of the mid-nineteenth century, when the diplomat and critic John Bowring commented: 'never has a country been so inundated with poetasters and doggerellers'. Since the 1880s, the progress of Dutch poetry has more often been a reaction *against* the previous generation than an homage to it.

But to return to our Flemish poet and his delayed influence. If *Hebban olla* were an arrow fired in the eleventh century and Dutch literature a train chugging towards the present, then this couplet from the late middle ages is an arrow of desire that landed in the Bodleian just as Anna Blaman was about to embark on her first lesbian novels, and twenty years before the artistic and social revolutions of the 1950s and '60s. So how much may *Hebban olla* have contributed to a culture that is as instantly recognisable, uber-individualist, and permissive as the Dutch? We can speculate on the degree because the question is beyond the strictly quantifiable. However, *Hebban olla's* timeless quality contains a quintessential Dutch yearning for hearth and home, as well as a frank sexual invitation, and reads like the building specs for the modern age, unfazed by war, holocaust and secularism.

But to return to Eros: the gay cruising spot in our city is the Rose Garden in the Vondel Park, named after the seventeenth-century playwright, Joost van den Vondel. There, the spent tissues lie among the shrubs like decapitated carnations. One can reasonably expect that there will have been a similar grove close to the abbey in Rochester, which may have been the catalyst for the composition of *Hebban olla* – as a declaration of love, or the arrangement of an assignation. But what relevance does the proximity of these two co-existent worlds have? It is actually the essence of Dutchness: freedom within a box, within a strictly delineated framework. There's even a noun for it: *verzuiling* (pillarization). It's no coincidence that Mondriaan was a Dutchman: his brightly coloured, clearly defined rectangles encapsulate both the landscape and the world-view of the people.

The home is often the theatre of experience for the Dutch, but can encompass a suffering akin to Rembrandt's *Slaughtered Ox*, as we can see in the work of Esther Jansma and Hester Knibbe. But the reverie of the inner gaze is not stifling; the Dutch are generally tabooless, morally unshockable. And their innate self-conviction feeds nicely into their artistic clean-slatism that is everywhere evident in this anthology. These ten poets, with a handful of others, were to dominate Dutch poetry from the 1980s and '90s into the 2000s, though with the exception of Jansma and Knibbe, none have yet had individual collections published in English.

The poet and critic, Rob Schouten, has written that Dutch poetry is a sponge that has absorbed all major movements, but that these are rarely coloured in a specifically Dutch way, and the Dutch are beachcombers scouring the coast for the bits they like. I'm not sure that I entirely agree, although it is the case that the Dutch are eager internationalists, transacting between larger cultures – with translation at the heart of their literary practice. But to test Schouten's hypothesis, let's consider the history of Dutch Modernism. Yeats commented that pre-war poetry had been living in a Tristan and Isolde dream-world until being shaken awake by The Great War and Eliot's sawdust restaurants. But where were these catalysts to Modernism in the Dutch-speaking world? The answer would give rise to a dual papacy on either side of 'the death wire' that separated neutral Holland from occupied Belgium.

To the south, the young Flemish cultural nationalist, Paul van Ostaijen was in Antwerp, a little the worse for wear from cocaine, as the city was occupied by the Germans. Although Van Ostaijen would end up sentenced for collaboration as a Flemish 'Flamigrant' nationalist, he was nevertheless an integral cog in the revolutionary European arts scene. He was greatly influenced by Apollinaire, DADA and Bauhaus; his multi-lingual, typographically expressionistic, hyper-modern diction was unlike anything that had appeared in the Dutch-speaking world. This from *Occupied City* (1921):

NIHIL   in crux suastika
    Nihil   in vagina
Zut   building cathedrals and shelling them
    blaming others
                naturally
                    citron nature
                others make babies
        vows of chastity are cheap

buggered and
blasted if we'll give
bishops generals statisticians the satisfaction
of counting children
Deo Gratias
    amen
(Translation David Colmer)

In contrast, the enchantment north of the death wire remained intact – here, it wasn't a case of fairy-tales or pastoralism, but a bourgeois self-contentment, maintained by neutrality in the unfolding apocalypse. And so, by 1917, we have the leading author, Nescio, writing 'In the year of the war, *Bellum transit, amor manet*' (war passes, love remains). Could Graves or Owen have written this in a stinking trench in 1917? It is reminiscent of Larkin's *Arundel Tomb*, an emotional distance that would be more appropriate far after the event. Nescio here has the tone of an erudite pavement-café writer. His writing echoes Henry James, it is an intelligent and wry depiction of the manners and mores of Dutch society at the turn of the Twentieth century. And so, lacking a seismic paradigm shift, it would take until 1934, and the publication of Martinus Nijhoff's *New Poems,* before we would witness a truly Modernist tone in Holland. In fact, many would maintain that the major revolution in Dutch literature was only brought about by the Second World War and the arrival of the new generation of experimentalist poets in the 1950s, although their work could be more accurately aligned with the Beats.

As for Nijhoff, he was engaged in his own journey from 'there is a captive animal beneath my skin', in 1924, to 'We were standing in the kitchen, you and me,' by 1934. Nijhoff had always been a restrained character, averse to the excesses of the 1880s, and he would hone a mature tone by the time he wrote his masterpiece *New Poems*, which contains the classic *Awater.* By now, Nijhoff had been struck by the rise of Eliot, although he was not *stylistically* influenced by him as such. Nijhoff's craft is more reminiscent of Yeats's *Responsibilities* period, and is evidence of the striking duality among the Dutch for the appreciation of the well-made on the one hand, and a baby-with-the-bathwater experimentation on the other. To illustrate, the seminal event in modern Dutch theatre is the Tomato Action of 1969, when the young theatre-makers pelted the actors at the City Playhouse who were performing Vondel's classic verse play, the *Gijsbrecht*: a debunking of the primary poet of the Golden Age that ushered in a theatre ruled by makers rather than writers.

By 1939, Nijhoff was opining that if he'd been writing in English, his international reputation would have been far more secure, and so he set the Dutch translator, Daan van der Vat, to work to produce an English version of the long poem *Awater*. It portrays a recently bereaved figure traipsing the streets in the wake of a nondescript clerk, who is associated with John the Baptist, and turns out to be a feted figure outside the 'office'. He finds himself called upon to perform a song at a restaurant (a translation of a sonnet by Petrarch). Rarely has a clerk enjoyed such celebrity. Nevertheless, Joseph Brodsky is correct in his estimation that this poem is a Modernist classic, although it is difficult to do it justice in English. In addition to existing translations, it may require a version with a music of abstraction similar to *Four Quartets*. ('Come unto me almighty ghost / That floats over the waters of creation. / Turn your fine eye upon this work, / Like the world it is waste and empty. / Unlike the whole of a previous century, it will not / Gaze upon ruins and sing of fine weather, / For singing is the suppuration of an ulcer / And whatever else it may have been it has never been / Ruins. The cornerstone has scarcely been laid / And each word renews the silence that it breaks.')

By the outbreak of the Second World War, Nijhoff was leading a bicycle squadron against the SS panzers. Holland would surrender within five days, and Nijhoff would soon be doling out bread from his own house to those suffering the deprivations of the Hunger Winter of 1944, and also advising on explosives for the resistance attack on the Amsterdam Population Register, where they kept the names and addresses of Amsterdam's 70,000 Jews. He also wrote for the underground paper *Free Holland*. In his own quiet way, he was as heroic as Camus at *Combat*.

The Second World War was the single most important event in modern Dutch history and is reflected as such in its fiction, if not its poetry. By May 1940, Holland was an occupied country where morality, loyalty and negotiating everyday life were one great grey zone of expediency, or resistance. The proportion of Jews deported from the Netherlands, with the active collaboration of the police, was higher than anywhere else in Europe; and de-classified government documents reveal that one in five Dutch citizens was actively spying for the Nazis. In contrast, there is a beautiful chain of dunes running along the west coast where members of the resistance were executed and dumped into mass graves. It is because of their sacrifice that a feel-good myth was able to take root in the Netherlands, in the absence of Truth and Reconciliation Committees. And so, by 1945, we have the poet J.C. Bloem writing *After Liberation*, this in Seamus Heaney's version:

> To have lived it through and now be free to give
> Utterance, body and soul – to wake and know
> Every time that it's gone and gone for good, the thing
> That nearly broke you –
>
> Is worth it all, the five years on the rack,
> The fighting back, the being resigned, and not
> One of the unborn will appreciate
> Freedom like this ever.

The mood of the post-war population was to return Holland to the pre-war status quo, including the poetry of the 1930s. But the younger generation were having none of it. There were two 'movements' afoot that would transform art, literature and society. These were the internationalist, experimentalist group of painters and writers, Cobra, (based in Copenhagen-Brussels-Amsterdam), and the loosely-affiliated 'Fifties' group of Dutch and Flemish poets. The painters were aiming for spontaneity, primitivism and bright colours, *à la* Joan Miró. Holland had scarcely been touched by Expressionism, Surrealism, etc., and the painters were looking for something beyond the limited Dutch palette. The poets, too, acknowledged no antecedence in the Dutch canon, but were more influenced by Michaux, Eluard and Artaud. They did, however, draw on the example of Van Ostaijen. They asserted Holland was dominated by the proponents of craft-for-craft's-sake and the 'completely dead sonnet'. There would be no more artificial separation between form and content, content would dictate form and punctuation was passé.

The 'Fifties' movement rapidly established itself as the only game in town. The group would produce three poets who would be influential over the next five decades – Lucebert, Campert and Kouwenaar. Lucebert was the self-styled 'emperor', a charismatic leader, a poet and painter. In the early days, he bridged the gap between the 'Fifties' poets and the Cobra movement. Many of his better-known poems have an in-built manifesto-like braggadocio ('I strive by poetic means/ that is to say / simplicity's luminous waters / to express the abundance / of life in its entirety'. Translation David Colmer), but his more interesting work has the inaccessibility and portentous musicality of Thomas's *Altarwise by Owl-light*. Lucebert would remain a central figure beyond his death in 1994. In 2018, it emerged that he'd been a Nazi volunteer and written anti-Semitic letters in his youth, which many of his admirers are still having difficulty coming to terms with.

After the early 1950s, Gerrit Kouwenaar developed from a socially-engaged experimentalist into the hermetic éminence grise of Dutch poetry. The poem was a 'thing' that possessed its own internal linguistic imperative. Sensory experience was still central – there are a lot of eating metaphors, for example – but the subjective 'I' was removed from the poems, to be replaced by the Dutch word 'men', which is halfway between 'you' and 'one', as he pursued the extinction of personality. This from his late collection *Total White Room* after the death of his wife:

One Still

One still needs to count the summers, to tender
a verdict, to render winter to blizzard...

...one still needs to disclose the blood stains to the
photographer
to untether from home, to change the ribbon in the
typewriter

one still needs to dig a grave for a butterfly
to switch father's watch for the blink of an eye –
(Translation P.C. Evans)

The 1960s would see a countermovement against the
experimentalists. The principal poets to emerge were Rutger
Kopland and Judith Herzberg. They gained wide readerships
among the general public, and critical plaudits. It would be
simplistic to describe them as anecdotal poets, but they did
deliberately root their work in accessible speech and everyday
experience – sitting out in the garden, studying a fly on the
window – but they invest the observed moment with great
pregnancy. Herzberg tends to strip the imagery and metaphor
out of her poetry, and replaces it with a musicality that
occasionally touches the Steinian ('...But the kiss / found a
caress / without hand / without cheek / ...A screech / of no
gull... / ...such a beach-combing / kiss will survive / by the
ebbing sea...' Translation Rina Vergano). Rutger Kopland, too,
had a gift for turning a simple *parlando* into philosophically
resonant ambiguity. The poetry often has a wistful yearning
for something apparently lost, but it is actually more an
unexpressed anthropomorphism of the present. Consider this
from his poem *Belvedere*:

I know those are woods, rivers,
meadows, villages, and that
I love them, I know it.
But more and more as now, as
a bird loves its nest:
not for ever. I see your withered
fingers on the rail, the small, grey
feathers fluttering at your temples,
the crowsfeet near your eyes…
(Translation James Brockway)

It may be surprising that a poet who is so evocative of nature considered the non-human to be soulless. When Kopland returned from hospital, he was surprised to realise how indifferent his beloved garden had been to him, where a number of his best poems had been set. It is clear that his suggestive ambiguity works best when plugged into traditional tropes of nature. When the technique is applied to a non-natural subject it can reveal its limitations. But Kopland left an oeuvre of great beauty, although since the 1980s, some of the younger experimentalists have once again reacted against it.

Eva Gerlach emerged in the late 1970s, a poet of the intense short lyric – formal, personal, but with a dark undercurrent. This from her second collection:

Vocabulary

This is your eyeball. This the sun. This cold
that tugs at you, is draught through the open window.
This water, where you will always fit in.

That is the kettle, that sings on the fire,
above the four knobs that turn on the gas.
That is the bread knife, plunged into the breadboard.

All of these things you must remember well.
Today or tomorrow they will have their way.
(Translation P.C. Evans)

However, her work has constantly re-invented itself. She would not consider herself experimental, but her poetry has undergone a dislocation of syntax and perspective under the pressure of a refracted observation of reality, leading to a sense of alienation ('It is strange the way it is with the dead/ …always they walk, meekly, / obediently, with their combs and their thorns their pelvic bone / over your genitals…/ tickticktick. Your skin alone / dampens their pressure a little').

Two poets who would emerge in the 1980s and '90s and dominate the next decades are Esther Jansma and K. Michel. Michel is comically, intelligently absurd. His images and phrase-making are perhaps the most startlingly original in the Dutch language. (from *Rule of Thumb*: 'If the house is infested, or so the saying goes / in the village that my grandparents called home / lock a pig in it for the night / and the bad spirit will crawl into it / and by morning the house will be clean // In the construction that each life is / a day will arrive that is known / as 'good advice doesn't come cheap'…).

Esther Jansma wouldn't have written poetry at all, but prose, if it hadn't been for an abusive mother who stung her in that direction. Jansma is a professor of Dendrology – identifying the age of wooden objects by growth rings in the wood. In her work, you can see the attitude of the investigative archaeologist, as she studies the layering of time, the enigmatic arrangement of the earth beneath our feet, the absurdity of possession and loss. But Jansma is also the archaeologist of the personal. In her collection *Time is Here*, she writes with excoriating lyricism of the death of her child:

from *Descent*

We crossed the Styx.
The ferryman lay drunk in his boat.
I took the helm and we sank like stones.

Water like the earth consists of layers,
transparent ribbons, glistening strata
of ever less life, less warmth.

Bubbles blossomed in your hair,
the current tugged your head backwards
and caressed your throat.

Stones waved with algae and ferns,
gurgled softly, sang of 'peace'.
They sliced your clothes away.

Fish licked the blood from your legs.
I held your hand tight. I wanted to comfort you,
but we were falling too fast and no words can exist

without air; …

(Translation James Brockway)

Amsterdam's poet laureate, Menno Wigman (who I have not translated) died in 2018 at the age of 51. Afterwards, I pulled up in front of his apartment block, to pick up a few books as mementos, and asked the next-door-neighbour if it was paid parking outside. "I've never heard of him", he said. I walked up the stone steps, three swastikas and the word 'bastard' were scrawled and half scrubbed out on his door; a review by a girlfriend, one would suspect. Inside, there was a full-length mirror, a litho from the 1890s of a young man in Gin Alley, lured into the bars by skeleton harpies, and a couple of thousand poetry collections. The Dutch Literature Museum had provided a subsidy for a researcher to record and photograph all of the dog-eared pages, to see which ones had influenced his work.

Ever the Baudelairean pessimist Wigman wrote:

> …it's not a *healing* art.
> The room remains a room, the bed a bed.
> My life's been wrecked by poetry and though
> I once had certain hopes, it won't go to my head
>
> if I, with these few sheets, disturb the peace of mind
> of sixty-seven readers or, worse, bring down two trees.

(Translation David Colmer)

Wigman shouldn't have been so downbeat, considering the hundreds at his funeral, and the weaponization of his words since his death. Recently, we have seen the rise of the populist far right in the form of the slick-haired proto-fascist, Thierry Baudet. He no longer talks of the Aryan race, but the superior

'Boreal' peoples. He likes to use Wigman's poetry at his events, as Trump did Elton John songs. Wigman's family have asked him to stop (what with him being a left-wing poet), but Baudet realises the power of poetry to mobilise precisely that type, like Wigman's neighbour outside.

EVA GERLACH

Eva Gerlach is a poet of the intense short lyric – formal, personal, and frequently with a dark undercurrent. She composes her poems under the pressure of a refracted observation of reality; the perspective is precise, disconcerting, alienating, but compelling.

VOCABULAIR

Dit is je oog. Dit is de zon. Dit koude,
dat aan je trekt, is tocht door het open raam.
Dit is water, waarin je altijd past.

Dat is de ketel, die op het vuur zingt
boven de vier draaiknoppen van het gas.
Hier zie je het broodmes in zijn plank staan.

Al deze dingen moet je goed onthouden.
Vandaag of morgen krijgen ze hun zin.

VOCABULARY

This is your eyeball. This the sun. This cold
that tugs at you, is draught through the open window.
This water, where you will always fit in.

That is the kettle, that sings on the fire,
above the four knobs that turn on the gas.
That is the bread knife, plunged into the breadboard.

All of these things you must remember well.
Today or tomorrow they will have their way.

*

Het was avond toen de mieren vleugels kregen.
In golven kropen ze uit de grond omhoog
en tegen het muurtje op; onwennig bleven
ze daar in het rond bewegen. Later vloog

een enkele soms tot de markies, maar waagde
de vlucht niet verder, viel of keerde terug.
Veel draaiden zich al dadelijk op hun rug.
Ook zag ik er, die aan hun vleugels knaagden.

*

It was evening when the ants sprouted wings.
They crawled in waves from their tunnels in the earth
and up a wall; awkward at first,
as they circled around. Later, they would fly,

one or two as far as the awning, but they wouldn't try
their luck any further that day. They fell away,
or turned back, many writhed upon their backs.
I even saw some gnawing off their wings.

DRUKTE

Het is raar gesteld met de doden,
schuiven in je aan, zitten met hun
holtes in je knieën, hun kootjes
in je vingers een brief te schrijven,
even sloom als jezelf, even beperkt op de hoogte
van weerbericht en genade, twijfel en kostprijs

en als het etenstijd, bedtijd,
tijd is om de honden uit te laten,
tijd om een kind te krijgen, een man te begraven,
altijd lopen zij, meegaand,
volgzaam, met hun kammen en doornen hun schaambeen
boven je geslacht hun schedelpan rond je
zinnen hun graat om je merg

in je door, tiktiktik. Alleen
je vel dempt hun drukte een beetje.

PRESSURE

It's strange the way things go with the dead,
always sidling into you, sitting with their
sockets in your knees, their digits
in your fingers, to write a letter,
just as sluggish as you, just as vague about the latest
weather report and mercy, doubt and the cost price.

And when it's dinnertime, bedtime,
time to let out the dogs,
time to bear a child, or bury a man,
they always walk, meekly
obediently, with their combs and their thorns and their pelvic bones
over your genitals their skulls around your
senses their spines around your marrow,

running all through you. Tickticktick. Your skin alone
dampens their pressure a little.

HOOR

De vrouw tegenover me heeft de hand van haar man
onder haar arm door gestoken en in haar
elleboogholte gelegd. Hij houdt haar vast

alsof ze er niet is. Hij hoort een vogel
zingen in de trein zegt hij, kanarie,
hoor je niet, hoor dan, zoekt hij in mijn hoofd
met dichte ogen, nee geen bandje, daar,

hun kind naast me kijkt naar het raam vol wit,
verbaasd om dat te zien, alles

te zien.

LISTEN

The lady opposite me has entwined her husband's
hand through her arm and lain it to rest
in the crook of her elbow. He holds on tight

as though she isn't there. He can hear a bird singing
in the train, he says, canary,
don't you hear it too, then listen, he's searching through
my mind, with eyes closed, it isn't a tape, no, there,

beside me, their child stares at the window that is filled with white,
astonished to see it, to see

all of it

ONDER HET VOUWEN VAN WAS

Ik lig in de kamer te sterven, kan nog lang duren.
Twee dochters vouwen was, de stapel groeit.
Ik heb altijd gedacht, zegt de oudste, dat niemand het meende

en dat het kiezen altijd door zou gaan,
je bent de melodie terwijl je speelt:

dat je dan kiest en alles rechtzet, maar.

AS THE WASH IS FOLDED

I lie there in the room dying, it might take a while.
There are two daughters folding the wash, and the pile grows.
I've always thought, the eldest says, that no one really meant

anything by it, and the choice would go on and on.
You are the melody as you play,

as long as you choose, and make everything right.

MIJN MOEDER LOOPT DOOR DE KAMER

Mijn moeder loopt door de kamer
op zoek naar een woord. Het woord heeft haar verlaten,
ze weet niet meer hoe het ging, de beweging ervan

in haar mond. Als ze het zei, begon alles
opnieuw, wat heel was kwam terug en
rampen maakte ze ongedaan want de tijd

kroop als een vogeltje in haar hand
en liet zacht op zich blazen, woord, woord, woord.
Hoe kun je de wereld veranderen als je het woord niet meer weet?

Meneer Touba haalt zijn schouders op. Hebt u de duizend?
Ga toch zitten, wat mompelt u toch.

MY MOTHER WALKS THROUGH THE ROOM

My mother walks through the room
searching for a word. The word's deserted her,
she doesn't remember how it went, the feel of it

in her mouth. When she said it, everything began
again, what had been whole came back and
she erased the disasters because time

crawled like a bird in her hand
and let her blow on it softly, word, word, word.
How can you change the world if you can't remember the word?

Mister Towba shrugs his shoulders. Have you got the thousand?
Do sit down, you do mumble a lot don't you.

STRAKS

Het was avond toen ik je losliet, het gat van je mond sloot.
Er bewoog niets meer in je, dat kon ik voelen want ik
hield je vast, dat mocht voor een keer.

Nu is het 05.40, december, stikdonker,
de krantenjongen gaat op zijn rammelfiets rond
en ik denk aan je als aan een woord dat ik bijna weet,

kan het niet zeggen maar het is er bijna, straks
wordt het in me naar binnen geschoven, dan sta ik op,
ga je kamer in, maak je wakker, dan ga je bewegen,

dan tellen we samen de woorden, die zijn er dan weer.

LATER

It was evening when I let you go – the hole of your mouth closed.
Nothing else in you was moving, I could feel it
because I was holding you tight, you let me for once.

It's 05.40. December. Pitch-black. The paper-boy's
doing his rounds on his ramshackle bike,
and I think of you like a word I almost know,

but can't quite say, it's on the tip of my tongue though. It'll come
to me later, and then I'll get up
and go into your room and wake you up, and you'll move,

and we'll tote up all the words, because that's when they'll be there again.

DE ZON EN ALLES

Iemand paste slecht op wat van mij was.
Gooide met mijn koffertje, scheurde
mijn boeken, verloor mijn jas.
Steeds meer wilde zij lenen en ik gaf
haar alles tot ik niets meer over had
in de verwachting dat het dan
wel goed zou komen, dat zij
rijk geworden voor mij zorgen zou
en ik zou niets meer doen en alles zou
vanzelf gaan. Maar het gebeurde
zoals je denkt, zij ging weg met de zon
en alles bij zich, alleen mij had zij
niet meegenomen. Aan het eind begon
het in die droom pas duidelijk
te zijn wie wie was, ik lichter dan ik.

THE SUN AND EVERYTHING

Someone didn't look after what was mine –
tossed my case, and tore
my books, and lost my coat.
She wanted to borrow more and more, and I gave
her all I had, till I had nothing more
to give. Expecting that then
everything would work out for the best, how having
grown rich, she'd care for me
and I wouldn't need to do anything and everything
would be as it should. But it all turned out
as you'd expect. She left with the sun
and with everything else. It was only me
that she didn't think to bring, and at the end
of the dream, it began to be clear
who'd been who, me lighter than me.

TEKST

Je had een gek gedicht bij je vannacht.
Vierkanten wit groeven in de bladzijde,
beeldschimmel knaagde aan de regelval,
cursieven gingen hun gang door de romeinen.
We braken onze ogen over het kleine
korps, ongelijk op het papier gebracht.

Aan water stonden we, ieder gelezen
woord vloeide weg als uit het vel losgekamd,
zonder ophouden keken we naar het lange
kalme stromen van haarscherpe zinsneden.
Toen werd het dag, ik zat hier met het lege
papier, waarvan je schaduw was verdwenen.

TEXT

You had a crazy poem with you tonight,
white furrows scored into the page,
the decaying images gnawing at the lines' fall,
the italics running scattered through the romans.
Our eyes broke on the tiny
corps, irregularly deployed upon the page.

We were standing at the waterside, each word
we read seemed to flow away from us
as if combed loose from a sheet. Without cease,
we watched the long, placid streams of sharp clauses.
Then day came. I sat here with the empty page,
from which your shadow had vanished.

GERRIT KOUWENAAR

Gerrit Kouwenaar was the socially engaged experimentalist of the 1950s, and later the hermetic éminence grise of Dutch poetry. The poem was a 'thing' that possessed its own internal linguistic imperative. His Eliotesque depersonalisation yielded his most striking poetry in the collection on the death of his wife, *Total White Room*.

DE STERFELIJKHEID HOUDT AAN

De sterfelijkheid houdt aan, deze morgen
ontwaakte er een in mijn slaap, en vanavond
vraagt het nuchtere glas om genade, men ademt
zich uit als een inzicht, men is, ik herhaal me

spel hoe men zich weervindt in dit haast vervleesde
voortdurend kortstondige zelvige grondstuk, lijf
lijk als weefsel, ik zijnde, wijn wikkend, zeker

de nachten zijn war en onzeker, verdichten zich
waar men in zit, men erft zich alleen
het steeds weer voorbije, zo tast men zijn omtrek -

MORTALITY IS INSISTENT

Mortality is insistent, this morning
someone woke from my sleep, and this evening
the sober glass pleads for mercy. I breathe out
as if that were an insight; one is, I repeat

myself, spell out how we again find ourselves
in this all-but fleshed out
familiarly fleeting plot of earth, as corporeal
as tissue, that would be me, mulling over a wine, for sure

the nights are chaotic and unsure, composing themselves
around you, while you inherit nothing
but the fleeting, and this is how you probe your environs

MEN MOET

Men moet zijn zomers nog tellen, zijn vonnis
nog vellen, men moet zijn winter nog sneeuwen

men moet nog boodschappen doen voor het donker
de weg vraagt, zwarte kaarsen voor in de kelder

men moet de zonen nog moed inspreken, de dochters
een harnas aanmeten, ijswater koken leren

men moet de fotograaf nog de bloedplas wijzen
zijn huis ontwennen, zijn inktlint vernieuwen

men moet nog een kuil graven voor een vlinder
het ogenblik ruilen voor zijn vaders horloge -

ONE STILL

One still needs to count the summers, to tender
a verdict, to render winter to blizzard

one still needs to pick up a few things before dark
asks one the way, black candles for the basement

one still needs to give sons a good talking to, to measure
daughters for armour too, to teach ice-water to boil

one still needs to disclose the blood stains to the photographer
to untether from home, to change the ribbon in the typewriter

one still needs to dig a grave for a butterfly
to switch father's watch for the blink of an eye –

IK HEB NOOIT

Ik heb nooit naar iets anders getracht dan dit:
het zacht maken van stenen
het vuur maken uit water
het regen maken uit dorst

ondertussen beet de kou mij
was de zon een dag vol wespen
was het brood zout of zoet
en de nacht zwart naar behoren
of wit van onwetendheid

soms verwarde ik mij met mijn schaduw
zoals men het woord met het woord kan verwarren
het karkas met het lichaam
vaak waren de dag en de nacht eender gekleurd
en zonder tranen, en doof

maar nooit iets anders dan dit:
het zacht maken van stenen
het vuur maken uit water
het regen maken uit dorst

het regent ik drink ik heb dorst

NEVER

I've never tried to do anything than this,
to soften stones
to draw fire from water
to draw rain from thirst

and all the while the cold was gnawing at me
the sun was a day swarming with wasps
the bread was either too salty, or too sweet
and the night was as black as it's meant to be
or white with its vapidity

sometimes I was confused by my shadow
as one might confuse a word with a word
a carcass with a body
day and night were often the same shade
without tears and stone-deaf too

but I've never tried to do anything than this,
to soften stones
to draw fire from water
to draw rain from thirst

it's raining I drink I'm thirsty

DAG VAN DE DODEN

Het is weer voorjaar, dag van de doden
maar het sneeuwde toen deze woorden zich schreven

zij schreven vandaag, maar nu zij zich spreken
sneeuwt het nog steeds op een doodstille stad

vandaag hoort de woorden de stilte bezweren
alsof de tijd ooit te stillen was

zij noemen zich bij onteigende namen
zij willen wat doodzwijgt verstaanbaar maken
en roepen omlaag en omhoog in een gat

en spellen de sneeuw die maar niet wilt smelten
op voorjaarsbloemen en monumenten
op vuilnisbelten en vazen met as

de witte stilte wordt gaandeweg grijzer
en wat de woorden ook willen ontzwijgen
de doden zijn dood, de bladzij is zwart –

DAY OF THE DEAD

It's spring again, day of the dead
but as these words were written, it was snowing

they wrote today as well, but now that they're spoken
it's still snowing on a deathly city

the day's listening as the words ward off the silence
as if time could ever be stayed

they name themselves by appropriated names
they wish to explain what still remains deathly
quiet, they cry high and low in a hole

spell out that the snow will not thaw
on the spring flowers or the monuments or
the heaps of rubbish and the urns of ash

the white silence grows slowly greyer
and what the words wish to utter
is that the dead are dead, the page is black –

HESTER KNIBBE

Hester Knibbe's poetry is intensely personal and direct, though without sentimentality, and she effortlessly combines the present with classical myth. The theme of loss is prominent, particularly in relation to the death her son at the age of 29 from a brain tumour.

Zelfs blind denk je nog alziende te zijn, maar
ziende was je al blind. In mijn armen draag ik
wat ik verdiende terwijl jij mokt, mij
tot zondebok maakt. Met open ogen

sliep je, nu zit je daar, sleet op de naad
van je kleed, een mol, het schoppen niet waard, jij
de rechtvaardige altijd goedgeefse, een vrek
bleef je, gehecht aan je macht. Nee

Tobit, ik ben geen dievegge, dat weet je,
tussen ons mekkeren alstu en danku, want
geven geeft achting, ontvangen maakt nietig, dát

zit je dwars. Was liever je ogen
met de gal die je spuwt, schrob de hoogmoedige
drek van je ziel. En zie!

ANNA RESPONDS TO TOBIT'S ACCUSATION

Even blind you think you're all-seeing, though
seeing you were already blind. There's nothing in these arms
but what I earned, and you just mope, make me out
the scapegoat. With your eyes open,

you were asleep, and now you sit there, the worse for wear
in a threadbare robe, a mole, not even worth kicking, you
the righteous, the never sparing, a skin-flint
that's what you are, clinging to control. No

Tobit, I'm no thief, and you know it,
given all the bleating of thankyou and please, for
it's nobler to give, demeaning to receive, and *that's*

what ticks you off. So why don't you wash out
your eyes with the gall you spit, and scrub the sanctimonious
crud from your soul. And see!

JA

Liefde, ja er zit altijd een lichaam aan vast
en dat maakt het en maakt het, maakt het

soms lastig. Maar het geeft niet, we zijn
al zo lang samen dat we ons in elkaar hebben
opgeslagen, niet meer zoek niet weg kunnen raken.

Natuurlijk, voorbodes kruipen onder de huid, dansen
mee als je danst, rennen mee als je rent, hangen

ook op de bank, zitten daar en later gaat Haper
aan de haal met je dromen, teistert een winter
de oude rivier die wil stromen. Maar het

geeft niet en de sfinx die ons het raadsel
opgeeft *wie van wie het meest* is niks

om je druk over te maken, we houden elkaar gewoon
bij de hand en waar de weg ophoudt zullen we slapen.

YES

Love, yes, there's always a body involved,
and that's what makes it and makes it, and makes it

so awkward sometimes. But it's ok, we've been together
for so long that we've filed ourselves away
inside each other – we can't lose sight of, or lose each other either.

Sure, the prognoses get under your skin, dance with you
when you dance, run with you when you run, hang

out with you on the couch, just sitting there, and later, Failure
will run away with your dreams, the winter will whip up
the old river that desires to flow. It

doesn't matter though, and the sphinx
that sets us the riddle of *which one of us the most* is nothing

to fret over, we'll just hold each other
by the hand, and where the road ends, we'll sleep.

ZOG

I

Nooit in fotolijstjes: koffers genomen
mijn jonkies daarin ondergebracht. Ze waren
te levend voor vreemde ogen, te luid
voor de stilte die rond mij

verwacht werd. Ik heb ze voortijdig
gered van gepest, doodtrap, uit het lood
gemept, want zoveel is zeker, leeuw en lam dat
gaat niet meer samen. Ik baarde

vormfout op vormfout, niet ontvankelijk verklaarden, een even
happen naar adem, terwijl mijn borsten oververzadigd
nee moeder nee moeder nee

begonnen te lekken. Bang verlangde ik
mij vast te klampen aan noodzaak.

A WEANING

I

I couldn't frame them, so I stowed
my little ones in trunks. They were too alive
for a stranger's eyes, too loud
for the silence they expected
to surround me. I was in the nick of time
to spare them being barged aside

by bullies. Because this much is certain, the lion
will not lie down with the lamb. What I gave birth to
was inadmissible, thrown out on a technicality.
That momentary gasp for air, and my breasts swelling,
no mother no mother no,

as they began to flow. Scared,
I longed to cling on to necessity.

*

Maar ik kon ze niet wegdoen daarom
heb ik ze in die koffers bewaard.

Want het is niet iets wat je zomaar
aan de buitenkant draagt, een T-shirt
broek die je zat wordt of slijt en

het is ook niet zoiets als nagels
en haren die je afknipt: wat je in je

droeg wil je niet kwijt. Vandaar dus
die koffers, een soort van op reis terug naar
een ander baarmoederdonker. Wat moesten ze nog

met licht in hun ogen dicht.

*

But I couldn't let them go, and that's why
I stowed them in the trunks.

They aren't like something you can wear
on the outside, a T-shirt or a pair
of slacks that you tire of, or wear out.

And they aren't like trimming your nails
or hair either, you can't sacrifice

what you carried inside you, which is why
I hang on to them. They're a voyage back
to the darkness of another womb. What else was there to do

with the light in their eyes after they closed.

2

Was ik een zeedier geweest met meer dan
zeven tentakels, ik had zonder bedenken
het stof van ze afgewaaierd zodat ze

konden ademen. Maar ik moest het redden met enkel
één hart wat hersens en deze twee handen.

Ik heb ze gekoesterd gevoederd gevoed met
gedachten aan later, maar iets in ze wilde niet
groeien, is lummelig misgegaan. Badwater te

warm of te koud, foute sokjes aan? Te weinig
of juist te veel doodgeknuffeld, haartjes te
kortgeknipt of te strak in vlechtjes gedaan?

Maar al wouen ze niet, ze moesten en zouen, ik heb ze
gelukkig gescholden gedwongen terwijl ik wel wist
hoe het leven je soms. Slavenwerk, dwangarbeid.

2

If I were a marine animal with seven tentacles
or more, I'd have fanned the dust from their faces
without a thought, so that they might

breathe. But I had to make do with nothing
but this one heart, this brain, these two hands.

I nurtured and nursed and nourished them with thoughts
of the future, but something inside them wouldn't grow,
they were crudely deformed. Was the bathwater too

hot, or too cold, were these the wrong socks? Did I coddle them
to death, trim their hair too short, or bind their braids too tight?

And whether they wanted me to or not, I made them, I
damned them to be happy, while I know
how life can be. It's slave work, hard labour.

3

Zo groot als hij was, een reuzenkind
hij zat in een kar en luisterde niet, had
vreemde verkeerde kleren aan en de wind
stak op, maar hij luisterde

niet, trok met een ouwelijk trage
hand een idiote geblokte puntcapuchon
over zijn blanco verwondering, zag
niet de paniek van zijn moeder

die riep: er is noodweer op komst. Hij
zat daar maar veel te niet bang, te grof ook
gebouwd voor een kinderkar: lemen

pop van bijna twee meter lang
die ik buiten adem leven inblies.

3

As big as he was, the gargantuan child,
he was sitting in his chair refusing to listen. He
was wearing these strange clothes when the wind
picked up, but he wouldn't listen.

His aged hand had tugged
down that idiotically checked hoodie
to cover his blank astonishment. He wasn't able
to see the panic in his mother's

eyes, who was crying – there's a storm coming. He
just sat there far too unafraid, too crudely
built for the chair: a clay

doll, almost two metres tall
that I'd breathlessly blown life into.

4

Slaap maar slaap in je baaierd van stilte
de bomen zullen je schaduw geven
een gazen koelte over je weven
en alles houdt de adem in.

  - mama hier zingen de vogels zo sober
heerst een zwarte seizoenloze zomer
bloesemt een overgrote verstrooiing

Je zonnige lachen staat op de foto
je prachtige lachen staat op de foto.

4

Sleep now sleep in the chaos of silence
the trees will cast a shadow over you
and weave their gauze of coolness too
and everything will hold its breath.

mama the birds here are singing so sadly
the summer is unseasonably black
the scattering of the blossom is so vast

Your sunny smile is captured in the photo
your beautiful smile is captured in the photo.

Ik zit in de kilte van steen.
Wit zijn de muren bedoeld, maar ze
breken, andere levens krioelen
erover, erdoorheen.

Op mijn schoot je marmeren lichaam.
Houd je ogen niet zo gesloten
wil ik je vragen, lach naar je moeder
sta op, wees wat lichter.

Nee.
Altijd zal ik je dragen.

You'll find me in the coldness of stone.
The walls were meant to have been white, but they're
crumbling, other lives are seething
over them, through them.

Your marble body is in my lap.
Don't shut your eyes like that
I should have asked, smile at your mother,
up you get, try to be a little lighter.

No?
Then I will always cradle you so.

HANS R. VLEK

Hans R. Vlek was the brilliant, arrogant, obnoxious rising star of the 1960s, with four prize-winning collections and a selected poems by the age of twenty-three. But a naked appearance at a poetry festival, and waving his gun at his publisher, may have hinted at mental health concerns.

He careered off the literary grid in the 1970s, as he divided his time between the brothels in Granada and the mental institution Bird Song, but he would return in the mid-80s with a sequence of collections that established him as one of the most original and compelling poets of the late twentieth century.

HET SONNET VAN ANGEL PASQUELITO, MANILLA

No dinero, geen geld. Elke dag met mijn jonger broertje
nog vóór donker naar de vuilnisbelt.
Daar vinden we rotte grapefruits, etensresten
van de stadsrestaurants en soms, voor mij, klein hoertje,

een oude nylonkous. Soms weinig, soms net genoeg.
Mijn broertje draagt de plastic zak, dan
breng ik hem weer thuis, nog vroeg. Vader heeft zweren,
moeder krijgt 'n zevend kind onder ons kruis met kaarsje.

Dan snel, snel, zo'n paar oude nylons aan en met
donker naar de drukke centrumstraten vol lichten en lokalen.
Daar geeft Jesús me voorschot om 'n toerist of 'n gringo uit 't
legerkamp te pijpen, genoeg voor verse vis en om olie voor de lamp

'n week lang te betalen. Ons land is het mooiste op aarde.
Je zou de maan boven de ochtendheuvels moeten zien! 'k Ben
al dertien!

ANGEL

No *dinero*, no dollars, no *baksheesh*. Each day before dark
Me and my *hermanito* hit the garbage heaps.
Sometimes we find some old grapefruits that we can eat,
Table scraps from chic downtown eateries, and for me

To work the streets, a pair of laddered tights. Usually, it's not much,
But it's enough. My *hermanito* scuffs the dust
As he dogs me with his plastic carrier. Then I whip
Him back early, cos pap's got ulcers, and mama's borne us a new sister

In the *barriada* beneath the candle and the cross.
Then it's *vamonos*,
Slip into a pair of the worn black fishnets
And cruise the cantinas on the scarlet streets at night.

Mama says that Jesus will grant a good girl dispensation
To blow a gringo from the army camp
And buy us fresh fish and oil for the lamp for a week or more.

I lie in the *desierto* beneath the Sierra Madre,
Where we played Hansel and Gretel among the desert magueys.
Mama, why did the soldiers take me, I am only thirteen.

KLEINE GESCHIEDENIS VAN DE LUST
...esse delendam.

Mithras had Mani de bedauwde druif verboden,
zelfs Augustinus, bij Hippo, verdedigde die leer –
Ook de bebilde perzik was uitsluitend voor de goden,
en de asperge, ach dames, vraag niet meer…

Fellatio en Cunnilingus, clowns uit 't oud Ostia,
gingen zwervend en vrolijk de platte globe rond,
Cunnilingus met 'n perzik, en de brave Fellatio
met 'n romige asperge in de geverfde mond –

Hippo werd 'n ruïne aan oudcarthaagse kust,
want 'n oudcarthaagse kust 't allerbeste,
als Tanit en Dido, en ten langen leste
is er sindsdien niets dan lust en lust
en luxuria, met drie vergulde ellen. En Ellen,
achter glas, zit neuriënd 'r geld te tellen –

A SHORT HISTORY OF LUST

...esse delendam.

Mithras had forbidden unto Mani the dewy grape,
Even Augustinus of Hippo defended the law –
The buttocked peach was only for the gods to take,
And the asparagus, dear ladies, ask of it no more...

Fellatio and Cunnilingus, clowns from Ostia, south of Rome,
Went roving merry the flat globe round,
Cunnilingus with a peach, and the good Fellatio
With a creamy asparagus in his painted mouth -

Hippo went to ruin on the old Carthaginian shore,
For an old Carthaginian shore is the best,
Like Tanit and Dido. And lastly, to rest,
There's been nothing since then but lust and more
Lust and luxuria, three gilded ells high. And Vi
Behind a window, humming as her money multiplies -

DE MEISJES VAN PORQ

Vergeef ze, de modellen van Porq met hun kontjes
van broderige billen en hun pruimpjes vol haar,
met hun volle borstjes waarop de tepelrondjes
't inferno vormen van de arme weduwnaar –

Ach, de meisjes van Porq, ze hebben uwe penis graag
van voren en van achteren, ze haten uwe pen.
Ze komen van Zodom zelve, 't Zodom van vandaag
en morgen, Daguerres pittoreske kippenren.

Oh, de kiekjens van Porq, goed voor de open haard
vol knetterend eiken en 'n dollar of twee.
Hun glanzende centerfolds mogen gespaard
door 'n Renoir of Hendrickloze van Rijn in spe –

Ach, de hoeri's van Porq, geef ze hun ferm deel.
Voer ze fótograven; oudere graven weten te veel –

PORQ

Forgive them, these models from Porq with their perma-tanned tushies
And their quims bristling with depilated hair,
With nipple-rings dangling from their silicon titties
To fire the inferno of the poor voyeur –

Ah, these girls from Porq, they like sir's penis,
From the front and from the back, but they hate sir's pen.
They may come from Sodumb itself, but they wave Gomorrah to
Ta-morra, from Daguerre's pictorial chicken pen.

Oh, the snapshots from Porq, good for the open hearth,
Full of crackling oak and a dollar or three.
Their gleaming centrefolds could have been set apart
By a Renoir or a Hendrick-less Van Rijn to be –

Ah, the tarts from Porq, slip them a generous portion.
Feed them with photographers, for what the undertakers know is just
    too awesome.

DE FEZZER SCHOENPOETSER

Een meester in 't knielen werd ik
toen de school voorgoed zich sloot.
Onder zon en palmen dien ik u
voor 'n schamel beetje brood,

wat mintthee en 'n sigaret.
Voor 'n vrouw heb ik geen geld, met
God en niets deel ik 'n eenzaam bed
en zie 'n leven lang toeristen

dure thalers tot nutteloze rommel kwisten
terwijl ik ga op oude, versleten sandalen.
Moge de God van 't goud u halen
en mij ooit kinderen schenken, huis en vrouw.

Een meester in 't knielen werd ik
toen de school voorgoed zich sloot.
En totterdood zullen m'n borstels trouw
de luxe dienen die 'k niet kan betalen.

Onder zon en palmen dien ik u
tot m'n anonieme trieste dood omdat
'k van 't leven nooit mocht proeven
omdat uw schoenen ijdele glans behoeven –

THE JUSTICE OF NARCISSUS

I was re-assigned as mistress
Emerita in the genuflection of the knee
When the academy was closed down permanently.
So beneath sun and cypress

I serve you, for a surreptitious cigarette –
Merci – a glass of mint tea and a crust of bread.
A nest egg? Hardly. I was never in the position
To get ahead, and being cursed with a mind and an acerbic tongue

Wasn't able to snag a husband and be his devoted wife.
So now, with God and nothing – ahem –I share a stoic's bed. And life?
It seems to be this centipede
Of sweaty apparatchiks milling before me,

Eager to haggle over the price.
I try to keep to the market line, I
Rarely cave. The gift of the gab comes almost as naturally
To me as it does to these cat-calling market furies.

But still a tutor to the marrow,
I can calculate this two-metre furrow
Of earth will be my universe until a death occurs,
And dust mixes with the dust.

But first, let this faithful rag burnish the reflections
In the brilliant mirror of your western
Shoes, and may I wish upon you, if
You can comprehend it,

The justice of Narcissus.

HET WONDER VAN HATTI EN HURRI

In Syrië ingemetseld op sommige hoeken der straten
vond men oude stenen met hittitisch hiëroglief

Eeuwenlang drukten oogzieke moslims het voorhoofd daartegen
eenvoudigen van geest kenners van het zangerig arabisch

In de hoop van bijziendheid en blindheid te genezen
drukten zij de schedel tegen het schrift der hittieten toen-

maals nog ongelezen en magisch geacht het hittiglief:
groot was het blind geweeklaag en hoofdbreken op de tekens van Hatt

Zo vond een oud Syrisch volksgeloof zijn bron in de bouwers
van hattushash en carchemish bouwers en hakkende schrijvers

En wellicht geneest ooit nog mystiek en mythisch dichten
velen van hun dogmatische staar naar rome jeruzalem en mekka

benares zelfs: de mannen en vrouwen van Hurri en Hatti
hielden een paradijs tussen de ogen geborgen

HEADBANGERS

Bricked into the cornices and quoins of some Syrian streets
One can still find a tablet carved with Hittite hieroglyphic reliefs.

For centuries, nomadic Islamists would press their crania against these
    baked clay bricks,
Simple spirits murmuring lamentations in a sing-song Arabic.

Hoping that by cracking their skulls on a foreign script
They could cure their myopia, or even blindness, and enter Utopia.

So, clearly, the source of this ancient Syrian superstition resides
With the brickies of the cities of Hattushash and Charchemish

And the chiselling Hittite scribes
– probably paid by the line –

And perhaps these mystical and mythical rhymes
–if they do indeed rhyme –

May have inspired the odd dogmatist or two
Into firing a prayer at Aleppo from Mecca

Or Jerusalem, or Rome – Who can say for sure
Whether the shades of the ladies and gents from Anatolia to Nineveh

May not have had their own bespoke picture of paradise,
Muzzled in the cross-hairs of the mind's eye,

As they are harvested like wheat in a mowing shoah,
A revelation of truth in a tongue of fire.

HANGMAT VOOR HENOCH

Bij rustend lam en Syrische leeuwen
tussen walnotelaars en geurende mandarijn
in 't tot hangmat verbouwde tempelgordijn
wiegt hij al zo'n veertig eeuwen,
neust ademloos in 't vergeten boek
vol precieuze schetsen van 't godsgezicht
– portretten van de schepper van Mardoek –
dat hem tot zalige euforie verlicht.

Er staan 'm nog reële trekken bij:
'n glimlach in ruisende donder
van 't hoge woord vloog 'm voorbij,
ooit, toen hij wandelde in wonder,

verre mijlen van waar hij lezend zwicht
voor dozijnen jakobsladders van 't licht –

Between the couchant lamb and the Syrian lions,
Between the walnuteers and the sweet-scented mandarins,
In a hammock converted from a temple curtain,
He has lain swinging for some four aeons,
Nosing breathlessly through the forgotten book,
Filled with precious sketches of the features
Of God – portraits of the creator of Marduk –
That rouse him to holy euphoric raptures.

Some of the real features are still fresh to his mind,
A smile amidst the ticking thunder
Of truth, that flashed through his mind,
Once, when he was wandering with his teacher in wonder.

Many miles from where he is devoutly decoding the papyri,
Detailing dozens of mi'rajes from the temple to the illuminati.

PARADE DER GODEN TE YAZILIKAYA

Duizenden hakten zweetten en hakten met harde bronzen beitels de
gebaarde statige koningen en krijgers aldaar een gigantisch filmdoek van steen

preperzisch passeren zij gevleugeld met trage trage arendswaaiers gedekt
gehakt door de mannen van Hatti de zwetende mannen van Hurri en Hatti

een zware lentewind van drieëndertig eeuwen doorstormt de aanblik
stevig en traag schrijden de koninklijke goden voorbij

Achter hen de tientallen krijgers met sikkels als cricketbats ter schouder
opgewekt conischgemutst dravend achter de majesteitelijke priester

Adem van een kapitale eeuwigheid bewaaiert er het bloed en zweet der turken
Ademloos stijgt de aanblik tot hooghemels zwaarmuzikaal zwijgen

BILDERSTURM

The power-tooled platoons are trimming and sanding,
The work gangs hacking and sweating and sweating and drilling,
Their jackhammers clacking like jackboots jabbing
On the plinths of the bearded Assyrian kings with their eagles' wings.

Don't stop for a ciggie whatever you do,
The foremen will be flicking their fickle
Sickles from Assyrians to Syrians
And they're looking at you,

While a film crew performs a collateral puppet show on the bas-reliefs,
Re-casting as a matinee idol a Portsmouth thief.
Smile and wave to the cameras for we are beautiful and we will never die.
Then the drill-bit continues to worm into the apple of Eden's eye.

DE HAARSPELD VAN FUJI

In de oude keizersstad Kyoto
tokkelde samurai Han-hon ooit droeve
slepende tonen op de drie snaren
van het geërfd, gelakte instrument.

Zijn geisha Fuji, een hitsig brok
en tevens diens Xantippe (gelezen had
de mikado uit boeken van Hollandse
mannen uit ver Decima) –

nam nooit haar haarspeld uit in bed.
Daarop schreef de samurai 'n haiku
als 'n dronken Ier z'n limerick:
'De hoge kreten van m'n Fuji,

als ik haar kreunende omarm!
Maar ach, heur haarspeld!'
Dit al in 17 Kyoter syllaben,
maar haiku verveelden hem snel.

Dan nam hij vlug een sake en 't
oude instrument ter hand, van vader's
vader ooit het rijkst bezit.
En bedacht iets voor de keizer. Maar

hoewel briljant van sentiment en wijs,
stuurde deze al Han-hon's liedjes terug.
Daarop greep de samurai Fuji, ontrukte
'r de speld, zij naakt hijgend op de rug –

SUBMISSION TO THE EMPEROR

Once in the imperial capital of Kyoto,
The samurai Han-San
Was picking a listless pizzicato
On his father's ancestors' shamisen.

His geisha Fuji was a fiery bint, and moreover
His Xanthippe. She'd read the Symposium
In the books of Dutch seamen
From distant Decima, and now would never

Take her hairpin out in bed, to let the wind-swept
Ripples of her hair cascade over the moonlit rocks of her hips,
No matter how he begged.
Until finally driven to the end of his wits,

The samurai knocked off five tankas as quick
As a shit-faced Irishman would a limerick,
And had them dispatched to the Emperor. But however
Brilliant, sincere of sentiment, or indeed wise, the Emperor

Had each and every one of the samurai's poems returned, with "Sorry"
Scribbled on a standard rejection note. Until he finally
Broke. And, having snapped, Han-San set off to mount Fuji,
Leaving in the dust the detritus of hairpin and poetry.

'T HEERLIJK HEITJE

'k Kocht 'n quinarius van Augustus met kleine kop
en achterop 'n engel met trofee, 'n juweel
van zeven millimeter zilver, onder de klop
van de hamer als gloednieuw vandaan, veel

zinsverrukkender dan de biljetten die 'k betaalde.
Dat halve dup schonk meer als 'n bestofte fles
Château Rothschild of krat champagne, en straalde
stil als 'n briljante kunsthistorieles
van stempelsnijders en orerende senatoren.

Zuiver was 't zilver, 'n antiek bazuintje klonk.
Octavio stond 'r, met grote messen gladgeschoren
in eeuwige jeugd op te lachen, en de lamp blonk
op 'n aanblik van twintig stoffigoude eeuwen.
Daarop begon 't legionairs te sneeuwen
en bezweette 'k herboren –

DE MORTUIS NIL NISI BONUM

I purchased one of Octavian's quinari
With its Janus face and on the reverse
An angel with a trophy. Struck
To bankroll the demise of that peacock Antony,
And Caesar's unflushable paramour,
By Divi Filius Gaius, Imperator.

Scene: a palace interior – enter a platoon of squaddies.
"First crack at the queen's cherry, three dinari, seconds
For two, but watch your arse with the myrrh and wine,
Or it'll be a cold coming in a dry passage."
Then a squaddie lays two pennies on her eyes for the passage.
"A queen's tithe for a good harvest."
Before he drains his serpent into the mouth of the blackening corpse,
And gives it a shake and tucks it away.
"Tell Caesarian, who will not live long, I guarantee
That she died a queen,
Her tits gagging for the viper's venom.
But to Agrippa only a word to the wise,
De Mortuis Nil Nisi Bonum."

LONGSTAY

De dames in 't paviljoen staren stil voor zich uit,
dommelen met 'n hoofd vol medicijnen op hun stoel.
In doodse stilte zitten ze zo weken te kwijnen, dag
in dag uit, bloemen staan voor niets hun best te doen.

Naar hun hel van spijt en eeuwig gemiste kansen
gaan ze zwijgend en slapend, zonder 'n klacht. Ze
hebben 't leven nooit begrepen, liefde nooit gekend.
Medelijden helpt niet meer als 'n rol chocoladeflikken.

Al was ik kristus of 'n boeddha en sprak: 'Kom,
grijze dochters, ook zonlicht is intelligentie, lach
om 'n boek en duik in de kunst als 'n bad': ze
zouden blijven staren bij een beker koude koffie.

Hun lauwe lethargie gaat 's morgens aan 't ontbijt
en 's avonds in het kliniekbed, tot niets bereid.

LONG STAY

The ladies in the pavilion are staring vacantly,
Dozing on their chairs, their brains dulled with pills.
They could sit there for weeks wilting, day in, day out,
The flowers try their best, but with no success.

Silent and soporific they go without complaint
To their hell of sorrow and all of their missed chances. They have
Never understood anything of life, never known love.
Compassion helps as little as a box of Smarties.

If I were Christ or Buddha, I'd say, come along
My grey daughters, even sunlight is intelligence, laugh
Over a book or dive into the arts like a bath. But they'd
Sit there staring by a beaker of cold coffee.

Their torpidity takes them to breakfast in the morning
And in the evening to the clinic's beds, prepared for nothing.

DE BLAUWZUURBLUES
for M.

'k Ben Abraham Weinstock, Uw laving,
ging door Belsens schoorsteen ooit omhoog.
Als museumdirecteur verspreidde 'k beschaving,
nu rust ik uit bij Jahvehs transen, en gedoog –

Mijn liefde voor de mens werd nooit begrepen,
m'n zwarte vilthoed altijd grenzeloos veracht.
Mijn hart, in zeven talen als veldspaat geslepen
vond kracht op Sinaï, waar me m'n schaduw wacht.

M'n dochter was 'n doorn in Goebbels' ogen,
haar neus te oosters, 'r Grieks te perfect.
Wagner en Nietzsche hadden voor 'r gebogen
had Arminius geen korporaal gebekt –

Maar boven de aarde is ons leven beter:
m'n Roemeense gade werd in Ravensbrück vermoord,
nu rusten we vredig in transcendente ether:
onze hora is vergeten en onze taal verstoord –

THE HYDROCYANIC BLUES
for M.

I am Abraham Weinstock, your servant,
Once through Belsen's chimney, I would rise high.
As museum director I spread refinement,
Now by Jehovah's battlements I rest and abide –

My love for my fellow man was never truly
Understood, my black felt hat always boundlessly despised.
My heart, through seven languages, as a moonstone borne with me,
Found its strength on Sinai, where my waiting shadow lies.

My daughter was a thorn in Goebbels' eye,
Her nose too eastern, her Greek too perfect.
For her, Wagner and Nietzsche would have stood aside,
If Arminius hadn't granted a corporal a ready wit –

But above the earth our life is better.
In Ravensbrück, my Romanian spouse was murdered.
Now we rest peacefully in transcendental ether,
Our hora forgotten and our tongue disturbed –

DIE MONOTHEISTISCHE RELIGION

Een oude dame in de trein leest Freud, en
Sigmund meent dat er geen god tot Mozes sprak:
hoe eenzaam moet zij uit het venster staren
met 'r vaderbeeld, 'r projectie, en 't vlak
uitzicht, zo plat als 'n ellenlang gedicht

tussen 't oude Groningen en ouder Maastricht,
waar wonderlijke wolken en kleinbespitste dorpen
voorbijgaan in dat goudeneeuws museumlicht –
De sappige weiden langs de Hollandse spoorlijn
zijn vruchtbaarder dan de Arcadische, en

't moeten wel deze brave gronden zijn:
de grazige weiden waarheen de Here voert,
waar men in naïef geloven vlijtig boert
en opziet naar die leerling van Charcot die
zo briljant uit z'n nekhaar oudehoert –

THAT MONOTHEISTIC RELIGION

The old lady on the train is reading Freud; there,
Sigmund proposes that no God spoke to Moses.
How lonely she must be as she sits and stares
Out of the window, with her father complex, her projection,
                                        and the featureless view
– as monotonous as an overly-long poem is –

Between the old burghs of Groningen and Maastricht, while
Wondrous clouds and small-spired villages pass by
In a Golden Age museum light –
The fertile meadows beside the Holland Railway Line
Are more fruitful that Arcady, and it has to be

These good grounds here, these
Grassy meadows where the Lord goes,
Where one with naïve beliefs industriously hoes,
And looks up to that pupil of Charcot, out of the back of whose
Head such amazing bovine extrapolation flows.

CANTO VAN PETRUS ROMERUS
...61 *AD*...
for M.

Als gepensioneerd Octaviaan gaarde
    'k een villa'tje bij Cartagena
na lang geknok tegen gedegen Galliër en ruwe Kelt.
Daar geniet ik met zonsondergang 'n vitamineuze cena,
niet onbemiddeld, zuinig op m'n fraaie kopergeld.

In m'n patio rust 'k bij roos en terracotta beker
- geschenk van een tribuun wiens namen ik vergat -
en schrijf er versjes, van de schoonheid zeker
als die malle Tertsarus in z'n zelfmoordbad –

Is m'n quintet geslaagd, stoof ik tonijn
In olijvezweet en herben, snuif zeezout daarbij.
Uiteraard nadien m'n beker flinkverdunde wijn,
en toe de cactusvijg met 'n ons amandelen.

Balba bracht m'n rollen ooit op Capri Tiberius',
maar die zwoer toen bij Vergilius' boerenrijmerij.
In plebstoga ga 'k nu 's avonds rustig uit wandelen,
geborgen m'n lied der grofgouden sestertius!

THE CANTO OF PETRUS ROMERUS
...61 *AD...*
for M.

As a retired Octavian I managed to procure
    a little villa near Cartagena,
After long struggles with the refined Gaul and raw Celt.
There at sunset I enjoy a vitamin-rich cena,
Not impecunious, careful with the copper coins in my money
    belt.

On my patio I rest by roses and a terracotta beaker
– a present from a tribune whose title escaped my mind –
And write verses, of beauty to be sure,
Like that fool Tertsarus in his bath of suicide –

If my quintet is a success, then I stew a little tuna
In the juice of olives and herbs, pinch a little sea-salt in.
Afterwards, of course, my beaker of heavily-watered wine,
And add an ounce of almonds and the cactus fig.

Balba once took my scrolls to Capri Tiberius',
But he swore by Virgilius's peasant doggerel rhymes.
I go out wandering in the evenings now in a plebeian toga,
Having concealed my song of the impure gold sestertius.

BALLADE VAN 'T BEEST

Bernd en Bertha, beiden bezig
't bordeel te boenen en te borstelen:
Bernd boent de bruine bar, Bertha
borstelt 't blauw behangfluweel –

Bernd en Bertha, beî uit Bremen,
bukken borstlend over 't bruin en blauw;
baas Bolle nog na beestachtig bacchanaal in bed.
Boven de bar bellen en bekers Babelsbräu.

Ballonnetjes blubber brengt Bernd naar 'n bak
bij de befbank, 'n bouwsel uit Boston
waar baas met 't biljart voor betaalde.
Bertha blanket de bruine borsten

van 'n bizar boegbeeld op die bronzen bier-
bron: 'n barokbouwsel op de bar.
Baas boert biljoenair en bol in bed,
Bertha bereidwillig de blaasbunny's nog ingevet –

Bernd boent 't bord: 'Bij de beste borrel
bieden wij blote billen' en bespuugt
z'n borstel voor diens betere blankte.
Bakken vol blubberballonnen bergt Bertha

naar buiten: 'Broemmm!' 'n beschilderde brommer
brengt beeldbladen naar buur en buitenwijk.
Babyblauw blikt boven de boulevard
de bahgeraad. Bernd brult Bertha naar binnen

THE BALLAD OF THE BEAST

Bernd and bertha, both busy
Buffing up and brushing the brothel.
Bernd buffs the brown bar, Bertha
Brushes off the blue velvet blinds –

Bernd and bertha, both from Bremen,
Bent brushing above the brown and blue;
Boss Bolle, after bestial bacchanal, still in bed
Above the bar, bells and beakers of Babelsbräu.

Bernd bears blubber balloons to the bin
By the blow bench, built in Boston,
Where boss bagged it with billiards.
Bertha blankets the brown breasts

Of the bizarre bust on the bronze beer
Taps with bleach, built in baroque style on the bar.
Boss, the bulbous billionaire, burps in bed,
Bertha obliging, the blow-up bunnies still greased –

Bernd buffs off the board: 'with the best beverage
We bring you bare buttocks', and blows
A gob upon his brush for the better brilliance.
Bertha buries bins full of blubber balloons

Outside at the back. Broommm! An emblazoned bike
Brings bright brochures to the burghers in the suburbs.
And baby-blue above the boulevard beams
The light of bawn. Bernd bawls for Bertha

en beî boenen ze bar en bordeel
bruin en blauw en boerenblinkend.
Bernd nog even snel 't bubbelbad boven
en de bordeauxbeklede bestiaalalkoven.

Beiden bennen bijna met de bizniz klaar,
behalve 't bergen van baas 'biefborstebil' op de bar

is bordeel nu bedrijfsbereid. Bernd en Bertha,
beiden beroerd betaald, begeven zich blij
naar buiten. Van boenen en bukken gebroken
banen ze zich naar de bushalte ter boulevard.

En babyblauw blikt de bahgeraad –

To come back in, and both of them buff the bar and the brothel
Brown and blue and barnyard beaming.
Bernd bolts up the stairs with the bubble bath,
And then turns to the Bordeaux-bedecked bestial alcoves.

Both beings being all but done with the bizzniz
But for the bearing of boss – beefbreastbuttock – to the bar,

The brothel is ready for business. Bernd and Bertha,
Both abysmally imbursed, disembark the brothel
With bliss. Broken by buffing and bending
They beat their way to the bus stop on the boulevard.

And baby-blue beams the light of bawn –

ROB SCHOUTEN

Rob Schouten is a poet and critic. He has translated Berryman, and similarly combines a formal excellence with an irreverent delight in skipping registers, wordplay and concocting neologisms. His work is laced with a subtle mocking irony, targeted both inwardly and outwardly.

OP TOURNEE

Op een avond strijk ik een overhemd
en ga een lezing over een collega houden.
Mijn god, wat een taal sla ik uit
over mystiek en reizen om er niet te zijn.
Hoe goed is het de dames te treffen!

En onder het kreukloos katoen
houdt mijn skelet mij overeind
waarin het met de organisatrice
genuttigd maal langzaam verpoept
in demi-sec pis van 1993.

Maar het helpt niet. De dichter is alleen
in het landschap van de geest,
zijn lekkere buurmeisjes ten spijt,
en hij reist niet om er niet te zijn,
hij reist om de reiskostenvergoeding.

ON TOUR

'For to travel hopefully is a better thing than to arrive,
and the true success is to labour.'
R.L. Stevenson

One evening I press a shirt
to go and give a talk on a colleague's work.
Christ, the shit I have to spout
about metaphysics and travelling being better than to arrive.
At least it's nice to see the ladies though.

And under this well-pressed cotton, my skeleton
keeps me straight, as it and the hostess grind
our dinner to *ordure*,
and one grows shit-faced by degrees
on a demi-sec piss circa 1993.

But, sadly, nothing helps, the poet is alone
in the landscape of the mind,
despite these delightful ladies flitting about.
And the poet doesn't travel because it's better than to arrive;
he travels only to declare the travel costs.

VROEGER

Lang geleden, maar wel na de oorlog
– Want die ken ik slechts van horen zeuren –,
Die tijd die heette toen het heden nog,
Kon het navolgende octaaf gebeuren:

'De huizen klappertandden met hun deuren,
In elke hoek zat een ontstellende Moloch
Jongens van mijn leeftijd te verscheuren
En aan mijn bed waakte een krom gedrocht.

Sliep ik bij toeval in, dan kwamen de Harpijen
Om elk tot bloedens toe met mij te vrijen
En 's ochtends knaagde een enorme beverrat

Aan alles wat ik op mijn lever had',
Omdat ik met het geld voor de collecte
Mijn potje voor dichtbundels spekte.

ONCE

Quite some time ago, but definitely after the war
– which I only learned about through word of moan –
At a time still widely known
As the present, the following octet happened to occur.

The doors of all the houses were clattering like teeth,
And in each corner lurked an unimaginable Moloch,
Waiting to get his hands on a young boy like me.
And indeed, at my bed loomed such an object of monstrosity.

I was having a lie in when the Harpies arrived,
Each to love me till I bled,
And by morning, they were feasting like outsized

Beaver rats on what had been running through my head.
Because I'd spirited from church his alms collection
To feather my own nest with a poetry collection.

DOORDEWEEKS

Over mijn authenticiteit gesproken,
belangstelling was er vandaag niet voor
en zelf lag ik half grieperig in bed.
Slechts één keer werd ik naar de deur geroepen
om aan auto-da-fe's mede te werken,
Getuigen van Jehova aan te steken.

Nietig gestemd bleef ik in kamerjas
urbi et orbi maar het raam uit staren
zonder veel wijzer van mezelf te worden
of van contemporaine wandelaars.
Nee, met de toekomst was het niks vandaag.

Avond werd het intussen wel natuurlijk;
pal boven mij werd smakeloos geneukt.
Om elf uur zei ik niemand welterusten
maar vals alarm, tot vier uur lag ik wakker
in knoedels laken en maar transpireren.

Ten slotte sliep ik mensen hatend in,
mijzelf ontpoppend als een stralend god
in een luchtig, niet te immens heelal
dat ik ineens ook weer verlaten moest.
Niets dat ik in de haast daar achterliet
en 's ochtends over was mijn griep ook niet.

WEEK DAY

As far as any authenticity may go
I couldn't generate much enthusiasm today.
Anyway, I was in bed half full of the flu.
I was only called to the door once
To participate in an *auto-da-fe*,
And to pass on the virus to a Jehovah's Witness.

I was feeling pretty shitty, so I spent all day in my robe,
Glowering out the window – *urbi et orbi* –
Without registering much mental activity, either towards myself
Or to the contemporaneous passers-by.
No, there was no future to be had today.

Darkness did arrive, of course,
And overhead someone was having a tasteless fuck.
By 11, I wished no one good night,
False alarm though, I'd lie awake till 4,
Tangled in sheets and sweating by the bucket-load.

I did finally nod off, but pretty misanthropically,
Only to re-emerge from my pupa like a beaming god
Into an airy, but not overly immense cosmos.
Soon to be evacuated once more,
Though not only because I had to scarper,
And come the morning, I still had my fever.

ONTGOOCHELING

Vandaag sprak ik iemand in wereldbeelden,
een oude opkoper die weinig bood.
Als je het kwijt wilt kan het niet veel zijn,
zei hij, en anders moet je het maar houden.

Hij sprak me moed in. Houd het, beste vriend,
wat denk je ervoor in de plaats te krijgen?
Het paradijs heb ik niet voor je bij me
en onder ons gezegd, het is er niet.

Maar ik hield aan, hardnekkig en wanhopig.
Wat biedt u, vroeg ik, slaap? krankzinnigheid?
vrouwen? mystiek inzicht? soms medicijnen?
de Zin? begaafdheid? misschien medelijden?

Geef het voor niets, zei hij - de vrek -, leven
is niet verplicht, dicteer een zelfmoordbrief,
die zal ik gratis voor je publiceren
totdat je iedereen hier interesseert.

- Er stonden mensen om ons heen te lachen.
Ik was hun tijdverdrijf, zij niet het mijne.
Loop door, riep ik, en ga me thuis bewenen,
of ruil met mij, dan lach ik jullie uit. –

Vergeet je jeugd, hernam de koopman kalm,
verspil je tijd niet aan afwezigheid
of aan oorzakelijk verband van iets.
Is er een muze, ga met haar naar bed.

DISENCHANTMENT

Today, I was chatting to someone in *weltanschauungen*,
A rag-and-bone man who didn't have much to offer.
If you're happy to part with it, it can't be much cop,
He said, and if it's not, you might as well hang onto it.

He gave me a slap on the shoulder. You just keep it, my old mucker,
What do you even think I'd give you for it.
I don't have the paradise you're looking for,
And between you and me…Well, you know the score.

But I kept at it like a dog with a bone.
What are you offering, I asked? Sleep? Madness?
Women? Mysticism? Insight? Herbotherapy maybe?
The meaning of life? Second sight? Or even pity?

I'll take it off your hands for free, he said – that wreck, life
Isn't an obligation, why don't you jot down your suicide note?
I'll publish it for free; maybe
It'll pique the curiosity of this gathering assembly.

– The people around us were only smiling,
I was passing their time, if they weren't mine.
Just keep on walking, I said, and don't dog me home like a funeral cortège.
Walk a mile in these shoes, and the one who'll laugh last won't be you.

Forget about your youth, the rag-and-bone man began,
Don't waste your time on what's long gone,
Or try to pinpoint a cause and effect.
If you've got a muse, why don't you take her to bed?

– die wil niet, zei ik - des te beter dan,
een eeuwige, maar sta niet bij haar stil.
Begin morgen opnieuw en overmorgen,
maak je geen zorgen over melkwegstelsels.

Verbitterd kwam ik thuis en dronk zeer veel
bij droevige muziek, ononderbroken,
tot ik stomdronken was en almaar dacht
dat ik louter mijzelf geschapen had.

Toen werd het zonder mij weer overdag
en onderscheidde ik mij op mijn kussen,
zonder noodzaak maar kennelijk ontwaakt
door iets inwendigs waar ik mee moest leven.

Ik ging de straat op en werd niet gelouterd
noch voelde ik mij wereldnieuws ineens
of nietig in de volle winkelstraten
of democratisch of tot iets verplicht.

De handelaar was weg, ik had een kater
uit duizenden en was naar niets op zoek,
maar vond het niet omdat er weinig is,
nauwelijks hoop en ook haast geen gemis.

– She isn't interested, I said; All the better,
She's a keeper, but don't keep hanging about.
Make a new start tomorrow or tomorrow
And don't fret about what the universe may dish out.

I got home, feeling pretty bitter, and decided to get hammered.
I put on a grim CD and hit replay,
Till I was three sheets to the wind and thinking,
What made me this way is me.

And yet with no assistance of mine, the sun rose the next day
To mark my chalk outline on the pillow, without rhyme
Or reason, but I was evidently awake anyway
And there was something inside me with which I'd have to deal.

So, I took to the streets, and didn't particularly feel
Purged, nor worthy of the international news,
But I wasn't nothing either on the busy shopping mews,
Neither democratised, homogenized, nor required to be anything at all.

The rag-and-bone man was long gone, leaving me with a hangover
For the ages and in search of nothing. And I failed
To find it because there's so little to be found, and nothing
To hope for, and nothing to miss that I'd particularly mind.

WILLEM VAN TOORN

Willem van Toorn is a poet and novelist. He is also the translator of Updike and Kafka, and was editor of the influential magazine *Raster*. In stark contrast to the experimentalism of the 1950s, his work has a restrained style, interwoven with gentle irony, as he paints the transitory individual in, and of, the landscape.

IN MEMORIAM

Ik droomde dat je naast me lag vannacht.
Je was al ziek. Je zei: tot in mijn merg
ben ik van dood. Vind je het erg
dat je niet in me kunt? Hou me maar zacht

tegen je aan. Ik zei: je was zo wit
en moe toen ik je zag – en dan onzicht-
baar in een kist waar ik het pad af ging,
de regen en het dorp in. Wachtend gras

lag naast de kuil in zoden opgetast.
Hoe ben je dan weer hier. Je zei: ik wou
nog doen wat ik waarom had nagelaten:
praten met je in bed hoe levens praten.
Maar wat ik nu ben heeft geen taal bij jou.

Er was geen lamp. Hoe ik je dan toch zag.
'k Viel in de droom in slaap. je hield me vast.
Koud bleef de kamer tot ver in de dag.

IN MEMORIAM

I dreamt that you were lying beside me last night.
You were already sick. You said, 'even my marrow
belongs to death'. 'Is it some kind of sorrow
for you that you can't come inside me? Hold me tight

to your side.' And I said, 'you were so white
and drained when I saw you', then you were out of sight
in that casket as I stumbled along the lane
and into the rain and the village beyond'. The waiting grass

had been hacked and stacked in sods beside the grave,
so how could you be here again. You said, 'I wanted
to do what I, God knows why, had always failed to do,
to chat with you in bed like living people do'.
But whatever I am now doesn't speak the same language as you.'

There was no lamplight, so how I might have seen you,
I can't say. I fell asleep in the dream and you held me tight,
and the room was cold till the end of the night.

V

Nu is het er, zie je wel, nacht
en ik droom misschien maar dat ik slaap,
want ik ben ook klaarwakker en vraag
waar hij mij heeft gebracht.

Maar hij staat niet meer achter
mij als ik omkijk. Ik ben
alleen in een lege straat
van een eindeloze buitenwijk.

Het regent niet, maar het lijkt
of dat wel zou moeten:
zo grauw de flats en plantsoenen
als in een naoorlogse film
die treurig afloopt.
   Wat of hij wil,
mijn onbekende kameraad
dat hij mij hier achterlaat
in een oude wereld zo stil

dat ik woorden in mijn eigen hoofd
hoor wakker worden? Maar dan zie ik plotseling
waar ik ben en wat hij met mij doet:
ik ben een flat in gegaan
en zie voor het grijze raam
mijn vader in zijn stoel.

Hij herkent mij weer. Ik ga naast
hem zitten en pak zijn hand.
Achter het raam is niets
alsof het huis in een wolk staat.

from THE RESERVOIR

V

There it is. I told you it would be. Maybe
the night and I were only dreaming
I was asleep because I'm wide awake now
and I ask him where he's taking me.

It's just that when I turn to face him,
he isn't there; I'm alone
in a deserted street
in an endless suburb.

There's no rain, but it feels
as if there ought to be.
The flats and city parks
are as grey as a post-war film
with a bad ending.

But what if this strange
companion of mine
were to decide to abandon me
in this ancient world, so still

that I hear nothing but the sounds of words misfiring
in my mind. Then I figure out
where I am, and where he's brought me.

I'm in a flat
backed up against a grey pane
and I can just about make out my father
sitting upright in a chair.

Zag je de paarden, lacht hij,
ze draafden in de Lingewei
alsof ze vlogen, de nevel
had hun poten gestolen
en wij hingen aan de manen,
jongens, voor de duvel niet bang.

Ik zeg, dat was vroeger, vader,
haast een eeuw geleden.
Hoe zou ik dat anders weten
dan uit jouw verhalen.
Maar van jou en mij samen,
wat weet je daar nog van?

Die oorlog van ons bijvoorbeeld,
een mensenleven lang
nooit echt voorbij. 'Vader, vader, er hangt
een brandend beest in ons raam,
kijk dan, het brult recht op ons af.'
Je droeg mij in je armen
trappen af en ik was
bijna niet bang meer. Dat was
toen je sterk was en nog lang niet dood
en ik dacht dat je god moest zijn.
Heb ik je dat ooit wel gezegd?

En weet je nog van de muziek,
Haydn, die je het liefst
draaide van al je platen,
de strijkkwartetten?
        Hij ziet
de vreemdeling die zijn zoon
moet zijn. 'Hadden we dan een grammofoon?'
zegt hij en zijn blik stroomt leeg.

He remembers who I am, so I sit down
beside him and take his hand.
Behind the window, there is nothing,
as if the house only exists in a cloud.

Do you remember the horses, he smiles,
how they cantered through the Lingewei
as though they were flying, the mist robbing them of their hooves,
and how we clung to their manes, boy,
and the devil took the hindmost.

But I say, that was such a long time ago, papa,
almost a century now,
and how could I even know
except for the stories you told.
But what do you remember of you and me?

The war between us that lasted maybe
a man's life long
and never really ended. Papa, papa,
there's a burning creature
dangling from the window, look,
it's bellowing at us.
You once carried me in your arms
down countless stairs, till
I was almost no longer scared.
You were so strong then,
Such a long way from death
and you felt like a god.
Did I never tell you that?

And do you remember the music
you used to play – Haydn,
your favourite LP,
his string quartets? He looks

Hij strijkt zijn hand langs zijn ogen
en dan is de stoel verlaten,
het raam vervaagt en de kamer
is onherroepelijk weg.

at the stranger
that his son must seem. Did we
have a gramophone, he says,
and the eyes run empty.
He draws a hand across them
and the chair is deserted.
The window clouds over,
and the room is lost forever.

TAFEL
Voor Gerrit Kouwenaar

Je denkt de dichter een tafel,
in een grenzeloze ruimte gedekt,
waarop moeder tijd, voor de heer
die hij ook altijd is, gul serveert
wat hijzelf van taal eetbaar maakte:

heuvels, akkers en dalen,
in de diepte de zilveren streep
rivier tussen blauwe wijngaarden
en het draaiende pad naar boven,
naar het huis met de fluisterende kamers
dat wacht met de ramen open.

Van aarde een troostrijke dis,
en dat het er waait, dat er licht
valt op grazige weiden
precies in de ene seconde
dat het oog fel en feilloos raak schiet.

Je wenst dat een herfstige tuin
zich voor hem opent op afroep,
met lelies die zich verheffen
als jonkvrouwen in de boomgaard,
en met gras dat geen voetstap vergeet
die zijn hand erin schrijft.

Je wil dat zijn tafel zo vol blijft.

TABLE

For Gerrit Kouwenaar

You picture a table for the poet, lain in infinite
space, where Mother Time serves
a feast to the host that he's always been
of whatever words he's prepared to eat.

Hills and fields and valleys
and in the depths the silvery seam
of a river between blue vineyards,
a path winding ever upwards
to a house with whispering rooms,
waiting with its windows wide open.

The consolation of Dis on earth,
as the wind rages and there is
light cast across fields of grass,
precisely in the single second that
the eye clicks fierce and unflinching.

And you wish him an autumn garden
revealing itself to him on command
with lilies rising from the ground
like young ladies seated in an orchard,
and grass that doesn't forget a single step
that the hand etches into it.

And most of all you wish him
a table that will always be so full.

Hoe een kraai vliegt over de heuvels bij Siena: een
   verkreukelde zwarte lap boven het koperen landschap.
   Werkt zich rot, denk je van onderaf, met die averechtse
   vleugels.

Door de kijker zijn slimme snavel, zijn eigenwijs hoofd: hij
   lapt het toch maar. Niet de begaafde vlechtwerken boven
   de stad van de zwaluwen - hij blijft een aardse

zitter, die heeft gedacht: waarom zij wel verdomme? en is
   opgestegen om zich verbaasd te begeven naar dit veel te
   grote blauw.

Hoe zich deze woorden bewegen ongeveer van mij naar jou.

A CROW NEAR SIENA

See the way the crow flies over the hillside at Siena,
a scrap of crumpled black cloth, skirting across
the copper landscape – it's working its socks off,

as you can see from below – its wings appear to work in reverse
as you watch it through the binoculars. Its brazen bill,
its bolshie brain, but he manages to pull it off.

Not for you, the aerial pyrotechnics of the swallows over the city,
and you will always be the terrestrial plodder
that thinks to itself, why them, for Christ's sake,
and rises – astonished – to steer towards the vast infinity of blue.

Just the way these words travel from me to you.

J. EIJKELBOOM

Jan Eijkelboom was born into a Dutch Reformed orthodox family. He served in the last Dutch colonial war, the 'police action' in Indonesia, and returned to the Netherlands suffering from panic attacks and nightmares. Through to the 1970s, Eijkelboom was a hard-drinking journalist and editor. He underwent psychotherapeutic treatment to deal with his alcohol addiction and PTSD.

He was also the principal translator of English-language poetry. Towards the end of his life, after suffering a series of epileptic fits and memory impairment, he was no longer able to write poetry, but would stand in the sun-lit window of his publisher's house in Dordrecht, watching his wife bring his children home from school.

ACHTERAF

Met moeite weet ik nog
dat ik je vreselijk kon haten
als ik je knoken hoorde kraken
op je te punctuele tocht
naar bed, en hoe ik vocht
om zelf maar niet in slaap te raken,
want wat ik van mezelf niet mocht
was alles wat jij niet kon laten:

de stipte plicht, het strikt geloof.
Hoewel ik toch mijn hoofd meeboog
voordat wij onze speklap aten,
want grieven wilde ik je niet.
Maar ik kon niet meer met je praten,
ik vreemdeling, die van je hield.

BLACK SONNET

With difficulty I still know
how terribly I could hate you.
If I heard your knuckles crack as it drew
to that too punctual hour for you to go
to bed; and how I fought so
with myself not to fall asleep, knew
that all of the things you couldn't leave alone
were things for which I had no use:

your strict code, your stern beliefs.
And though I bowed my head when we
sat at table to eat our bacon,
because I didn't want to hurt you,
I could no longer talk to you then.
I, the stranger that loved you.

LEGE KERK

I

Het hoog karkas, de nutteloze ruimte,
preekstoel en orgel afgedekt, een leegte
die het licht naar binnen zuigt.

De jongen die daar zat op bikkelharde,
nu weggehaalde banken, verzon eens
hoe je slingerend van lichtkroon

naar lichtkroon als Tarzan kon ontkomen
aan 't herderlijke dwangbevel
dat onder hem de kudde deed verstarren.

Wat bleef is een afwezigheid
die heel die ruimte vult en reikt
tot aan het tongewelf, het schedeldak

van wie hier staat en ongeschonden
straks weer het heiligdom verlaat.

II

Anderzijds zijn de zerken
zolang buitengelegd, gestapeld
als de lijken die ze eens dekten.

De zerken zelf kwamen bloot
toen de planken vloer werd gelicht.
Toch zijn ze drastisch versleten,

EMPTY CHURCH

I

The tall carcass, the useless space,
organ and pulpit covered, an emptiness
that sucks the light into it.

The boy who sat there, on the rock-hard
and now-removed pews, once imagined
how like Tarzan, you could swing

from chandelier to chandelier, and evade
the pastoral compulsions
that stiffened the flock beneath him.

What remained is an absence
filling the whole space and stretching
to the barrel-vaulting, to the cranium

of one who stands intact here
and will shortly leave this sanctuary behind.

II

The tombstones, on the other hand,
have just been stacked outside, dumped
like the bodies they once covered.

The tombstones themselves were only laid bare
when the planks of the floor were taken away.
Yet, they are terribly worn,

althans wat er was aan reliëf: wapens,
festoenen, alsook de bolle wangen
van putti, hun eens zo dartele geslacht

tot een puntkomma afgevlakt; alleen
wat werd gegrift is nog wel leesbaar
maar niet meer van belang.

at least what there was of relief: the arms,
the festoons, the chubby cheeks
of cherubs, their once perky genitals

eroded to a semi-colon; only
what was inscribed can still be read
but is no longer of any importance.

GELUID

I

Betekenissen
zijn voor woorden te talrijk
maar gaan zelf onder
in zeeën van geluid.

De componist haalt er zijn klanken uit
maar luistert naar veel meer.
Endlich fortissimo, riep Mahler
naast de Niagara.

Maar wie heeft dat verstaan?
Hij die het opschreef
zodat het voortleeft:
het vastgelegde woord
en het gesproken woord
zijn niet geheel overbodig –
dat zult u mij nooit
horen zeggen.

II

John Cage stond in een echoloze cel
en hoorde twee geluiden.

Het hoge was zijn zenuwstelsel,
het lage was zijn bloedsomloop.

Er is geluid zolang je leeft,
er zal geluid zijn na je dood.

SOUND

I

For words, meanings
are too multifarious,
they merely sink beneath
oceans of sound.

The composer trawls the tones out
but he listens to much more.
Finally, *fortissimo*, cried Mahler
at Niagara.

But who can understand this?
The one that wrote it down
so that it continues to live:
The recorded word
and the spoken word
are not entirely superfluous –
This, you will
never hear me say.

II

John Cage was standing in a sound-proof cell,
listening to two tones.

The higher was his central nervous system,
the lower the circulation of his blood.

There will be sound as long as you live
and sound after you die.

Voor de muziek, schreef Cage in Silence,
is er daarom nog alle hoop.

For music, Cage wrote in Silence.
There is, after all then, still hope.

WIJZIGING VAN UITZICHT

Het uitzicht nu teruggebracht tot dit
uiteinde van een pannendak,
een hemel door de wirwar
van een vergeten tv-antenne.

Het hoge raam desnoods te bereiken
per ladder, maar waarom?
Het zit vast als de muur
waarin het vervat is.

Maar het laat licht door van boven
dat uit de eeuwigheid kon komen
als men daarin geloofde.

Soms valt het op een hand, een vuist,
een prop erin die kermen wou
maar niet veel verder kwam
dan ritseling.

Dan weer raakt het een hoofd
dat opkijkt en ziet:
daar is het luchtpostblauw.

Het brengt hem iemand te binnen
die lavendel fijnwreef
en toen haar vingers
onder zijn neus hield.

Nooit eerder
was er zulk een bescheidenheid
van de wellust.

A CHANGE OF PERSPECTIVE

The view now reduced
to this end of a tiled roof,
the sky through the barbed wire
of a desolate TV antenna.

The high window to be reached if needs be
by ladder, but why?
It's as much of a dead-end
as the wall it's cemented into.

But it does let the light in from above
that streams out of eternity
if you believe in all that.

And sometimes it falls on a hand, a fist,
that clutches a crumpled scrap
that tried to groan
but got no further than rustling.

Then it strikes a head
that looks up and sees
there is air-mail blue

bringing someone to mind
who once ground fine lavender,
holding her fingers
beneath his nose.

No one has ever known
such modest anticipation
or indeed such desire.

WIE SCHRIJFT GESCHIEDENIS

– je liep daar naast mij
in je gouden jack. –
(21 november 1981)

Ligt er ergens nog dat jack, van goud
dat toen al was gaan slijten?
Door barsten zag je mosgroen leer.

Hoe anders liep ik naast je
dan toen ik tussen andere soldaten
marcheerde met mijn schietgeweer.

Andere oudgedienden
schreven toen in de lucht:
Ga toch in Moskou demonstreren.

Wie schrijft geschiedenis?
Niet zij die met hun lichtste voeten
meelopen in bevlogen stoeten.

Maar ook niet de benarde heren
die vanuit burcht of binnenhof
een vloedgolf denken te dicteren.

Een dagje mensenzee. Of was het meer?
Een ommekeer of nieuwe wijn
voor oude poëzie? Ik weet alleen:

Gelukkig liepen wij toen, daar,
verliefd op honderdduizend mensen
en ook nog op elkaar.

WHO WRITES HISTORY

Do you still have that golden jacket,
which even then was peeled and worn?
You could see the cracks through the moss-green leather.

How different it felt to walk alongside you
than when I was marching in a column
of soldiers, shouldering a rifle.

Now, the other old servicemen
are writing in the air:
go demonstrate in Moscow.

Who writes history?
Not anyone whose lightest steps
clack together in a well-trodden parade.

And also not those critical gentlemen
who from citadel or chamber
would think to dictate to a tidal wave.

An outing of the human sea?
Or was it more?
A new beginning or fresh wine
for old poetry. I only know

we were happy then as we walked together,
in love with a hundred thousand people,
and with each other.

H.H. ter Balkt's work is rooted in the rural eastern Netherlands, but it also incorporates history, the visionary and the disparate contemporary. Ter Balkt's principle was that the poem must be in, and of, the modern world, or it is nothing at all. He responded to this flux by consistently re-writing his poems, so that we are left with multiple versions of many of his best-known works.

1800

De honderd steden met poorten 's nachts op slot.
In de grachten, tollend van vuil, roeit de bacil
van cholera asiatica aan. Venen tussen de steden
dof overstromend. Droge gronden hoeden jager en

herder. Aan de oostgrens rondom de dorpen weiden;
akkers met meekrap, vlas, hop, hennep. Laagveen
daalde in 't water af. Soms, in de mistflarden, bij
vuurvliegjes, dwaallichten, zweeft als uit een bijt

gehakt, ivoor, het oudste beeldje aan van een eerst
gezicht, haar hals omlijst door geplooid doek boven
de laatste wolf en bever. Haar neus ruikt de geur

van het onland, pinksterbloem en zuring. Drijfnat,
hard en onherbergzaam zijn duister toevluchtsoord
grijze dorpen; koud volkje zit bij houtrook en vuur.

1800

A hundred cities with their gates closed at night.
And in the canals that are churning with filth, the bacillus
cholera asiatica starts to stir. The marshes between the towns
are completely submerged. And the dry earth

is under the purvey of the hunter and herder. On the eastern border,
the villages are ringed with heaths and fields of madder
flax, hop and hemp. The fens too have slipped into the water. And sometimes,
in the streaks of mist, fireflies, will-o'-the-wisps, the first face drifts

like an icon hewn from ice or ivory, the throat
ringed with a crumpled cloth, as it hovers over
the last wolf and beaver, the nose sniffing the scent

of marsh, lady-smock and sorrel. And in this darkening
harbourage of grey villages, it's pelting it down, inhospitable,
and the cold folk hunkers in the wood-smoke and fire.

HAKSELMACHINES OP DE HORIZON

Schapen niet meer: enkel de geslepen wolf.
Op de horizon herkauwen onmerkbaar
hakselmachines wat hun invalt. Binnen
blikkeren de aquarellen; 't zijn vissen

met graat en al rauw afgedrukt op de steen.
Zelfs de Rijn is misschien ook een vorm van pijn
zoals voeten en stemmen, lang vergeten
wat hun dreef. (Vierde-monden, halve kelen.)

Sneller dan avondwolven is de vijand
die op ons jaagt: 't is in een dode-zeerol
dat dit nog staat. Op een Stèle van Miró

brandt een ronde zon boven wat een landschap
lijkt, en met een rivier. Als gesternte straalt
wat blijvend moet zijn, in de wereld en ons.

THE SHREDDERS ON THE HORIZON

No more sheep now, only the cunning wolf.
And on the horizon, the unlamented gnawing
on whatever happens to be fed into the shredders. And inside
the aquarelles glitter like fish,

their spines pressed into the fresh clay.
Maybe the Rhine is a form of pain too
like those long-forgotten feet and voices, and
what drove them on, those jubilant mouths, those half-choked cries.

But what's swifter than the wolves at evening
is the enemy pursuing us. This was written
on a Dead Sea scroll. And one of Miró's Stéle too –

the round sun burns over what seems to be
a landscape, a river. A constellation glimmers
over what has to endure, of the world and us.

DE STOFSLIERT EN DE VLIEGTUIGMAGNEET

'Ik
sta op'
Ahmad Shamlu

De stofsliert met de drakenkop
die in de luchtstroom slingert
wordt niet moe te herhalen 'Stof
zijn we, alleen slingerend stof'

Enkel aan de levenden zendt nog
de vliegtuigmagneet zijn tijding
'Wantrouw 't sprekend stof altijd
en 't worstmolentje dat geest maalt'

Aan de standbeelden van fijnstof:
'Hooiland, dat is jullie gebieder
Niet elke stem is van een mens,
in de aastijd van lachende spoken'

Gekloonde fantomen ratelen dof
hun echo's en mantra's af; velden
vol troepende hooiers, en in zee
jakkert de muil van de koekjeshaai

In de landen van de blinden zwijgt
nu de eenogige, als de Krakatau
in de Ijsvogeltijd van Apollinaire,
de verkondiger van de koude eeuw

Fantomen roepen neergang af want
fantomen willen neergang en slaap
Buiten waait de wind, kinderen en
oh schaapskudden, blijf op de been

THE RIBBON OF DUST AND THE AIRPLANE MAGNET

'I
quit'
Ahmad Shamlu

The ribbon of dust with the dragon's head
that flitters in the current
never tires of repeating, 'Dust,
that's what you are, nothing but flittering dust.'

These days, the airplane magnet sends its tidings
only to the living,
'Always mistrust the talking dust
and the meat-grinder of the soul.'

And, to all of you monuments of dust, 'Wheat fields,
this is your Lord speaking,
not every voice has to be a human voice
in this carrion age of grinning ghouls.'

The cloned phantoms are dutifully rattling off
their echoes and their mantras; the fields
are full of trooping threshers. And in the sea,
the jaws of the cigar-shark feed mechanically;

In the land of the blind, the one-eyed
man is as shtum as Krakatoa
in Apollinaire's kingfisher times
– that harbinger of a colder age.

The phantoms are crying for the decline and fall,
for phantoms desire nothing but decline and sleep.
Outside where the wind is howling, the children
and flocks of sheep just run and run.

GA UIT DE ECHOKAMERS

…Kanker carnaval van het vlees,
kermis van 't lijf niet ziel genaamd
ziehier bij stil weer
enkele scherp geslepen komma's.

…Virussen stampten in mijn voorhoofd
als arme Samojeden,
mijn achterhoofd daarentegen
knarste van lijpe dragonders.

…Mijn muts schutse en hut.
Aan de muur de wetsteen.
Krakende karren, blinde voerlui
daalden het Ertsgebergte af.

Ga uit mijn waterwingebieden,
ga uit de echokamers;
daar resideert niet de hartslag,
daar klopt de hamerslag.

Dieven leegden de klokken
en toch loopt de vlier weer uit;
de blinden in hun vertrekken
zetten een nieuwe schreeuw op.

Oh Hannover en gestapeld land!
Agricola vertrok naar Mainz,
op Kruittorens stuiten bruggen
en het ongeluk eindigt.

CLEAR OUT OF THESE ECHO CHAMBERS

Cancerous carnival of the flesh,
AKA the fairground of the carcass not the soul.
Look, when the weather's clear,
you can pick out a handful of sharpened commas.

The viruses are pounding in my forehead
like pitiful Samoyeds,
and at the back of my head
is only the grinding of a platoon of moronic dragoons.

Under my skull-cap, the haven and the harrying.
And on the wall the whetstone.
Blind coachmen with their creaking carts
are crawling down the Ore Mountain Ridge.

Clear out of the water basin,
clear out of the echo chambers.
You won't hear a heartbeat here. Here,
you'll hear only the hammer-blow.

The thieves may have bled the clock dry,
but still the elder spreads its vines.
And in their various quarters the blind
have struck up a new lament.

Ah, Hannover with your shipping-crate hinterland,
Agricola has decamped to Mainz.
The bridges are clattering at the powder towers,
as the accident comes to an end.

K. MICHEL

K. Michel is by turns intelligently absurd, comical and philosophical. His images and phrase-making are the most startlingly original in the Dutch language. He was also an editor of the influential magazine *Raster*, and has translated Octavio Paz.

NEE EN JA

Nee en ja er is altijd
meer dan één keus
En voor je iets doet (of laat)
kun je altijd tot basta tellen.

Een ruzie vraagt twee meningen
een kus vier lippen
een lichaam vijf liter bloed

Om regen te maken. een boom
een huis, muziek, een droom
zijn meerdere elementen vereist

En in de sporen van schichtige dieren
rond een modderige drinkplaats
schitteren 's nachts ontelbare sterren

Voor iemand die slechts denkt
met één (en niet de ander)
is dat getal een hamer
en is de hele wereld een spijker.

YES AND NO

You'll always have yes and no
More than the one choice to make
And before you do that (or don't)
you can always count up to *finito*

A quarrel requires two points of view
a kiss four lips
a body five litres of blood

To make rain, a tree
a house, music, a dream
you require a number of elements

And in the tracks of furtive beasts
circling the muddy waterhole
the countless stars gleam by night

For those who think
in one (but not the other)
the number is a hammer
and the whole world is a brass tack

DOMINO

Er zwemt een barst door het huis
Niemand die luistert

Uit de schaduw groeien schaduwen
in het onderwaterlicht
dat passerende auto's werpen
op de muren rondom het bed

In de diepblauwe stilte
herhaalt een jongetje lipzacht
al wat gezegd is die dag
en stopt woord voor woord
de gaten in het geluid
dat huwelijk heet

De vloer golft
De deurklink is ver

En het jongetje houdt zijn handpalmen
als een boek in zijn handen
en ik lees 'kom terug, ga weg'

Een spreuk, een dominosteen
die een ster slaat
in het glas van mijn huis

Dan begint het buiten
bruidsjurken te sneeuwen

DIE

There's a fissure swimming through the house
and nobody's listening

In the shadows, shadows grow
in the sub-aquatic glow
cast by passing cars
upon the walls around the bed

And in the deep-blue silence
a little boy softly replays
all that was said that day
and word for word, he stitches
the holes in sound
known as marriage

The floor is a quivering wave
The handle of the door far away

And the boy spreads his palms
as if a book is in his hands
and I read 'come back, go away'

A fairytale, a die
that strikes the glass of my house
and leaves its star

while outside, bridal gowns
of snow begin to fall

VUISTREGELS

Is het woonhuis besmet, zeiden ze
in het dorp van mijn grootouders
sluit dan een varken een nachtlang op
het kwaad kruipt in het beest
en alles is de volgende morgen schoon

In het bouwsel dat elk leven is
breekt er een moment aan dat heet
goede raad was duur, een lekkage
heeft de muren bedekt met rorschachfiguren
en het ruikt naar iets dat ooit
tijdens een oud spelletje werd verstopt

Kijk de tafel rond en probeer
uit te vinden wie de sigaar zal zijn
zo luidt een gouden tip voor pokeraars
zie je het slachtoffer niet
dan rest er maar een mogelijkheid

Dus zeg ik deze nieuwe dag
tegen het gezicht in de scheerspiegel
stop met graven als je in de put zit
wees bereid au & ja te zeggen
kijk om je heen, doorzoek alle kamers
en vind je het varken niet
dan ben jij het

RULE OF THUMB

If the house is infested, or so the saying goes
in the village that my grandparents called home
lock a pig in it for the night
and the bad spirit will crawl into it
and by morning the house will be clean

In the construction that each life is
a day will arrive that is known
as 'good advice doesn't come cheap'. A leak
will have daubed the walls with Rorschach forms
and there'll be a reek of something once
stashed away in a distant game

If that is the case, take a look around the table and try
to figure out who the shmuck may be
which is a golden rule for a poker player
and if you can't make out who the mark might be
that leaves just one possibility

So on this new day I say
to the face in the shaving mirror
if you find yourself in a hole quit digging, know
it may be time for you to say ow & ok
take a look around, rifle through every room
and if you can't find the pig
it's you

ESTHER JANSMA

Esther Jansma is a professor of Dendrology – identifying the age of wooden objects by growth rings in the wood. In her work, you can see the attitude of the investigative archaeologist, as she studies the layering of time, the enigmatic arrangement of the earth beneath our feet, the absurdity of possession and loss.

HET IS TE VINDEN AAN DE BINNENKANT

Je vindt me mooi? Ik ken de kou van mij
in de uiterst aandachtige adem van mijn maakster
liggen schamen. Nooit was ik genoeg.

Die blik van haar. Haar handen die maar deden:
het is niet goed, we doen er oortjes op,
smelten er voetjes aan, schuren het met zand

totdat het glanst, we scheppen er de ziekte uit
en branden het in vorm tot het iets is
dat glad en sierlijk op zichzelf kan staan

en pijnloos zwijgt, definitief, liefst in de schaduw
van een kamer – wie langsloopt en toevallig
ernaar kijkt, moet denken: fijn, daar is het voor.

Ik ben dit niet. Ik zit verscholen op de plek
waar ik geboren ben als mest en stro
in de holte onder de mascara van mijn gepolijste

glasdraden die zij tot slot om ook de laatste
wilde vreemde onooglijke resten van mij
uit te wissen, volstopte met nachtzwart.

YOU'LL FIND ME ON THE INSIDE

You think I'm pretty? I know this cold inside me,
I've felt nothing but shame in the terribly attentive
breath of my maker. I was never enough.

That look of hers, her hands which never quit,
this isn't any good, let's stick some ears on it,
mould feet on and sand it down

until it gleams. Then we'll scrape out the sickness,
and burn it into a form, until it's smooth
and elegant and can stand alone

in pain-free silence, definitive, and preferably
in the shadows of a room – so whoever happens to walk by
and glance will think, fine, that's what it's meant for.

But this isn't me. I'm concealed in the place
I was born as dung and straw,
in the core beneath this mascara of glazed

glass coils. And to finally expel
the last wild, strange and distasteful remains
of me, she pumped it full of night-black.

DE VAL

We kruisten de Styx.
De veerman lag dronken in zijn schip.
Ik hield het roer en we zonken als stenen.

Water bestaat als de aarde
in lagen, transparante linten, glanzende strata
van steeds kleiner leven, minder warmte.

In je haren bloeiden luchtbellen,
de stroom trok je hoofd naar achter
en streelde je hals.

Stenen wuifden met armen van algen en varens,
zongen zachtjes gorgelend 'vrede'.
Ze sneden je kleren los.

Vissen likten het bloed van je benen.
Ik hield je hand vast. Ik wilde je troosten
maar we vielen te snel en er zijn geen woorden

die zonder lucht bestaan, mijn liefde
bleef boven, blauwe ballonnen, bakens voor even,
de plaats markerend van het ongeluk

voordat ze verder dreven. Je mond ging open.
Je gezicht werd rood, je handen zochten
evenwicht, zochten mijn armen.

Je probeerde in me omhoog te klimmen.
Je was een glasblazer met een wolk van diamanten
aan zijn mond. Ik hield je vast als een katje.

THE FALL

We crossed the Styx.
The ferryman lay drunk in his boat.
I held onto the rudder and we sank like stones.

Water, like the earth,
is composed of layers, transparent ribbons, gleaming strata
of ever less life, less warmth.

Air bubbles bloomed in your hair,
the current eased your head back
and stroked your throat.

Stones waved their arms of algae and ferns,
and softly sang of gargling 'peace'.
They slit your clothes away.

The fish licked blood from your legs.
I held your hand tight. I wanted to comfort you,
but we were falling too fast, and no words

can exist without air, my love
was above, blue balloons, brief flares
that marked the site of the accident

before they were swept on. Your mouth fell open,
your face grew red, your hands sought
balance, sought my hands.

You tried to climb inside me.
You were a glassblower with a cloud of diamonds
around your mouth. I held you as tight as a kitten.

Ik aaide je vingers.
Je liet niet los.
Je sliep en ik aaide je vingers, liet los.

I stroked your fingers.
You wouldn't let go.
You fell asleep, and I stroked your fingers, let go.

LITERALS

EVA GERLACH

Vocabulary

This is your eye. This is the sun. This cold / that tugs at you is draught through the open window. / This is water, in which you always fit. //

That is the kettle, that sings on the fire, / above the four knobs for the gas. / Here you see the bread knife standing in its board. //

All of these things you must remember well. / Today or tomorrow they will have their way. //

(*Double meaning: the last line can also be read as 'Today or tomorrow they will get their meaning'*)

*

It was evening when the ants got wings. / In waves they crawled up out of the ground / and up a little wall; they kept / circling around there awkwardly. Later, //

a few flew as far as the awning sometimes, but didn't / risk the flight further, fell or turned back, / many quickly turned onto their backs. / I even saw some that were gnawing at their wings. //

Pressure

It's a strange state of affairs with the dead, / They shove into you, sitting with their / sockets in your knees, their digits / in your fingers, writing a letter, / just as sluggish as you, just as limitedly informed / about weather report and mercy, doubt and cost price. //

And when it's dinnertime, bedtime, / time to let out the dogs, / time to have a child, or bury a man, / they always walk, meekly / obediently, with their combs and thorns their pelvic bone / over your genitals their skulls around your / senses their spine around your marrow, //

all through you. Tickticktick. Only / your skin dampens their pressure a little. //

(*Double meanings: the title means both 'pressure' and 'commotion'; 'only' also means 'alone' in Dutch because of the line break*)

Listen

The woman opposite me has stuck her husband's hand / through her arm and lain it in / the crook of her elbow. He holds her tight //

as though she isn't there. He hears a bird / singing in the train he says, canary, / don't you hear, then listen, he searches in my head / with closed eyes, no not a tape, there, //

their child next to me looks at the window full of white, / astonished to see that, to see //

everything //

While washing is folded

I lie in the room dying, could take a while. / Two daughters are folding washing, the pile grows. / I've always thought, says the eldest, that no one meant it //

And the choosing would always go on. / You are the melody as you play, //

as long as you choose and make everything right, though. //

My mother walks through the room

My mother walks through the room / in search of a word. The word has deserted her / she doesn't remember how it went, the movement of it //

in her mouth. When she said it, everything began / again, what had been whole came back and / she erased the disasters because time //

crawled like a bird in her hand / and let itself be blown on softly, word, word, word. / How can you change the world if you can't remember the word? //

Mister Touba shrugs his shoulders. Have you got the thousand? / Do sit down, you do mumble don't you. //

Later

It was evening when I let you go, closed the hole of your mouth. / There was nothing else moving in you, that I could feel because I / was holding you tight, that was allowed for once. //

Now it is 05.40, December, pitch-black, / the paper-boy is going around on his rickety bike, / and I think of you like a word that I almost know, //

can't say it but it is almost there, later / it will be slid into me, then I'll stand up, / go into your room, wake you up, then you will move, //

then together we will count the words, they will be there again then. //

The sun and everything

Someone badly looked after what was mine. / Threw my case, tore / my books, lost my coat. / Ever more she wanted to borrow and I gave / her everything till I didn't have anything left / in the expectation that it then / would work out well, that she / having grown rich would care for me / and I wouldn't do anything more and everything would / go as it should. But it happened / as you would think, she went away with the sun / and everything with her, only me she had / not taken along. At the end / in that dream it began to be clear / who was who, I lighter than I. //

Text

You had a crazy poem with you tonight. / Square white grooves in the page, / image decay gnawed at the lines' fall, / italics went their own way through the romans. / We broke

our eyes on the little / corps, irregularly applied to the paper. //
At water we stood, every read / word flowed away as though
combed out of the sheet, / without stopping we looked at the
long / calm streams of hair-fine sentence clauses. / Then it
became day, I sat here with the empty / paper, from which
your shadow had disappeared. //

(*Double meaning: sheet (of paper) and skin are the same word*)

HANS R. VLEK

The sonnet of Angel Pasquelito, Manilla

No dinero, no money. Every day to the rubbish dump /
before dark with my younger brother. / There we find rotten
grapefruits, food scraps / from the city restaurants and
sometimes, for me, little whore, //

an old nylon stocking. Sometimes little, sometimes just
enough. / My little brother carries the plastic bag, then / I
take him home again, still early. Father has ulcers, / mother's
having her seventh child under the cross with candle. //

Then quick, quick, put on a pair of the old nylons and go / in
the dark to the busy central streets full of lights and drinking
establishments. / There Jesus gives me dispensation to give a
blow-job to a tourist / or a gringo from the army camp, enough
to pay for fresh fish and oil for the lamp //

for a week. Our country is the most beautiful on earth. / You
should see the moon above the morning hills! I am / already
thirteen!

A short history of lust
  …esse delendam.

Mithras had forbidden Mani the dewy grape, / even Augustinus, at Hippo, defended the doctrine – / The buttocked peach was also only for the gods, / and the asparagus, ah ladies, don't ask more… //

Fellatio and Cunnilingus, clowns from old Ostia, / went roaming and cheerful around the flat globe, / Cunnilingus with a peach, and the good Fellatio / with a creamy asparagus in the painted mouth – //

Hippo became a ruin on the old Carthaginian coast, / because an old Carthaginian kisses the very best, / like Tanit and Dido, and finally / since then there's been nothing but lust and lust / and luxuria, with three gilded Ls. And Ellen, / behind glass, sits counting her money as she hums – //

(puns: *'coast' and 'kiss' are the same words in Dutch; as are 'Ls' and 'Ellen'*)

The girls from Porq

Forgive them, the models from Porq with their bums / of bready buttocks and their twats full of hair, / with their full breasts on which the circles around the nipples / form the inferno of the poor widower – //

Ah, the girls from Porq, they really like to get your penis / from the front and from the back, they hate your pen. / They come from Sodumb itself, the Sodumb of today / and tomorrow. Daguerre's picturesque chicken-run. //

Oh, the snapshots from Porq, good for the open hearth /
full of crackling oaks and a dollar or two. / Their gleaming
centrefolds may be spared / by a Renoir or Hendrickless van
Rijn to be – //

Ah, the little whores from Porq, give them their firm portion.
/ Feed them photographers; older counts know too much –

(Pun: *the word 'counts' is a play on photographers/gents/graves*)

The Fez shoeshine

I became a master in kneeling / when the school closed down
for good. / Under sun and palms I serve you / for a meagre bit
of bread, //

some mint tea and a cigarette. / I have no money for a wife,
with / God and nothing I share a lonely bed / and see tourists
my life long //

wasting valuable thalers on useless junk / while I go around on
old, worn-out sandals. / May the God of gold come for you /
and someday grant me children, house and wife. //

I became a master in kneeling / when the school closed down
for good. / And till death my brushes will faithfully / serve the
luxury that I can't afford. //

Under sun and palms I serve you / until my sad anonymous
death because / I was never allowed to taste of life / because
your shoes require a vain shine – //

The miracle of Hatti and Hurri

In Syria, bricked in to some street corners / one found old
stones with hittite hieroglyphs //

For centuries, Muslims with eye diseases pressed their
foreheads against them / simple souls who knew the song-like
Arabic //

In the hope of curing shortsightedness and blindness / they
pressed their skulls against the Hittite writing then //

still unread and considered magical the hitti-glyphs: / there
was much blind wailing and breaking of heads on the symbols
of Hatti //

And so an old Syrian popular belief found its source in the
builders / of hattushash and carchemish builders and hacking
writers //

And perhaps sometime mysticism and mythical poetry
writing will cure / many of their dogmatic stare towards rome
jerusalem and mecca //

even benares: the men and women of Hurri and Hatti / held a
paradise safe between the eyes //

Hammock for Enoch

By resting lamb and Syrian lions / between walnut trees and
aromatic mandarin / in the temple curtain converted to a
hammock / he's already been rocking for some forty centuries,
/ breathlessly nosing in the forgotten book / full of precious

sketches of the face of god / − portraits of the creator of Marduk- / that enlighten him to divine euphoria. //

He can still recollect real features: / a smile in roaring thunder / of the word from on high flashed by him, / once, when he wandered in wonder, //

distant miles from where he's reading and keeping silent / about dozens of jacob's ladders of light − //

Parade of the gods at Yazilikaya

There thousands hacked sweated and hacked with hard bronze chisels the / bearded stately kings and warriors a gigantic film screen of stone //

pre-persian they pass by winged covered with slow slow eagle's fans / hacked by the men of Hatti the sweating men of Hurri and Hatti //

a forceful spring wind of thirty-three centuries storms through the sight / strong and slow the royal gods stride past //

behind them tens of warriors with sickles like cricket bats at their shoulders / in conical headgear excitedly trotting behind the majestic priest //

Breath of a capital eternity fans the blood and sweat of turks / Breathlessly the gaze rises to heavenly high heavily musical silence //

Fuji's hair-pin

In the old imperial city Kyoto / the samurai Han-hon was
once plucking sad / lingering tones on the three strings / of
the inherited, lacquered instrument. //

His geisha Fuji, a hot-blooded piece / and also his Xantippe
(who'd read / the mikado in the books of Dutch / men from
far Decima) – //

never took her hair-pin out in bed. / Thereupon the samurai
wrote a haiku / like a drunken Irishman his limerick: / 'The
high-pitched cries of my Fuji, //

if I embrace her moaning! / But, ah, her hair-pin!' / All this in
17 Kyotee syllables, / but haiku quickly bored him. //

Then he quickly took a sake and the / old instrument in his
hand, once / the richest possession of father's father. / and
thought up something for the emperor. But //

however brilliant of sentiment and wise, / he sent all of Han-
hon's songs back. / Thereupon the samurai grabbed Fuji,
snatched / the pin off her, she panting naked on her back – //

The delightful bob

I bought a quinarius of Augustus's with a little head / and on
the back an angel with a trophy, a jewel / of seven millimetres
of silver, from under the rap / of the hammer as if brand new,
much //

more of a delight to the senses than the bills I paid. / That half a dime gave more than a dusty bottle / of *Château Rothschild* or a crate of champagne, and still / gleamed like a brilliant history lesson / of die-cutters and orating senators. //

The silver was pure, an antique trumpet sounded. / Octavio was standing on there, smoothly shaven with big knives / smiling in eternal youth, and the lamp shone / on a sight of twenty dusty-old centuries. / Then it began snowing legionaries / and sweaty, I was re-born – //

(Double meaning: *that half a dime gave more / poured more like*)

Long stay

The ladies in the pavilion are staring ahead motionless, / dozing with a head full of medicines on their chair. / In deathly silence they sit like this for weeks withering away, day / in, day out, flowers are standing there doing their best for nothing. //

They go to their hell of sorrow and eternally missed chances / silently and sleeping, without a complaint. They / have never understood life, never known love. / Pity helps no more than a roll of chocolate buttons. //

Even if I were christ or a buddha and spoke: 'Come, / grey daughters, sunlight is intelligence too, laugh / about a book and dive into the arts like a bath': they'd / keep staring by a mug of cold coffee. //

Their lukewarm lethargy goes to breakfast in the morning / and in the evening in the clinic bed, prepared for nothing. //

That monotheistic religion

An old lady in the train is reading Freud, and / Sigmund is
of the opinion that no God spoke to Moses: / how lonely she
must be staring out of the window / with her father image,
her projection, and the flat / view, as flat as an interminable
poem //

between the old Groningen and older Maastricht, / where
miraculous clouds and small-spired villages / pass by in that
golden age museum light – / The luscious meadows along the
Holland Railway Line / are more fertile than the Arcadian,
and //

it must be these good grounds: / the grassy meadows where
the Lord leads, / where one in naïve belief diligently farms, /
and looks up to that pupil of Charcot who / so brilliantly yacks
out of his neck-hair – //

The hydrocyanic blues
 for M

I am Abraham Weinstock, Your servant, / once went up
through Belsen's chimney. / As museum director I spread
refinement, / now I rest by Jehovah's battlements and endure
– //

My love for humanity was never understood, / my black felt
hat always boundlessly despised. / My heart, in seven languages
polished like a moonstone / found strength on Sinai, where
my shadow is waiting for me. //

My daughter was a thorn in Goebbels' eyes, / her nose too

eastern, her Greek too perfect. /
Wagner and Nietzsche would have bowed for her, / if Arminius
hadn't given a corporal a big mouth – //

But above the earth our life is better. / my Romanian spouse
was murdered in Ravensbrück, / now we rest peacefully in
transcendental ether: / our hora is forgotten and our tongue
disturbed – //

Canto of Petrus Romerus
  ...61 AD...
  for M.

As a retired Octavian I gathered together / a little villa near
Cartagena, / after long brawls against refined Gaul and raw
Celt. / There at sunset I enjoy a vitamin-rich cena, / not
impecunious, sparing with my fine copper money. //

On my patio I rest by rose and terracotta beaker / - a present
from a tribune whose names I forgot - / and write rhymes, of
beauty to be sure, / like that foolish Tertsarus in his suicide
bath - //

If my quintet is a success, I stew tuna / in olive sweat and
herbs, pinch sea-salt in. / Afterwards, of course, my beaker of
heavily-watered wine, / and after the cactus fig with an ounce
of almonds. //

Balba once brought my scrolls to Capri Tiberius', / but he
swore then by Virgilius' peasant doggerel. / In a pleb's toga I go
for a quiet walk in the evening now, / my song of the impure
gold sestertius concealed! //

Ballad of the beast

Bernd and Bertha, both busy / polishing and brushing the brothel: / Bernd polishes the brown bar, Bertha / brushes the blue velvet wallpaper – //

Bernd and Bertha, both from Bremen, / bend brushing over the brown and blue; / Boss Bolle, after bestial bacchanal in bed. / Above the bar bells and beakers of Babelsbräu. //

Bernd brings balloons of blubber to a bin / by the licking bench, a construction from Boston, / where boss paid for it with billiards. / Bertha blankets the brown breasts //

of the bizarre figurehead on the bronze beer / tap: a baroque construction on the bar. / Boss burps billionaire and bulbous in bed, / Bertha obliging the blow-up bunnies still greased – //

Bernd wipes the board: 'with the best beverage / we offer bare buttocks' and spits on / his brush for its better brightness / Bertha puts away containers full of blubber balloons //

outside: 'Broommm!' A painted moped / brings glossies to neighbour and suburb. / Baby blue the boulevard beams / above the bawn. Bernd bawls Bertha //

back in and both polish bar and brothel / brown and blue and country beaming. / Bernd quickly upstairs with the bubble bath / and the Bordeaux-bedecked bestial alcoves. //

Both beings almost ready with the bizniz, / except for putting boss 'beefbreastbuttock' on the bar, //

the brothel is ready for business. Bernd and Bertha, / both badly paid, happily go / outside. Broken from polishing and bending / they make their way to the bus stop on the boulevard. //

And baby blue beams the bawn //

GERRIT KOUWENAAR

Mortality persists

Mortality persists, this morning / one woke in my sleep, and this evening / the sober glass asks for mercy, one breathes / out like an insight, one is, I repeat my //

game how one again finds oneself in this almost flesh-like / continually fleeting self-like piece of earth, bodi- / ly as tissue, being me, weighing wine, sure //

the nights are confusing and unsure, compose themselves / where one is at, one inherits only / what is constantly the passing, thus one probes one's periphery //

(*Kouwenaar constantly uses words with multiple meanings, and draws out further layers of meaning through his line endings. For example, 'game' also means 'to spell', 'bodi-ly' means both 'like a corpse' and 'alive', etc.*)

One must

One must still count his summers, to pass / his sentence, one must still snow his winter //

one must still do shopping before dark / asks the way, black candles for in the basement //

one must still give courage to the sons, measure / the daughters for armour, teach ice-water to boil //

one must still show the photographer the blood pool / withdraw from the house, change the typewriter ribbon //

one must still dig a pit for a butterfly / swap the moment for his father's watch – //

I have never

I have never attempted to do anything but this: / to make stones soft / to make fire from water / to make rain from thirst //

meanwhile the cold bit me / the sun was a day full of wasps / the bread was salty or sweet / and the night as black as it's meant to be / or white with ignorance //

sometimes I confused myself with my shadow / as one can confuse the word with the word / the carcass with the body / often day and night were coloured the same / and without tears, and deaf //

but never anything else than this: / to make stones soft / to make fire from water / to make rain from thirst //

it is raining I drink I am thirsty //

Day of the dead

It's spring again, day of the dead / but it was snowing when these words wrote themselves //

they wrote today, but now that they're speaking / it's still
snowing on a deathly-still city //

today hears the words warding off the silence / as if time could
ever be stopped //

they name themselves by expropriated names / they want
to make what keeps deathly-silent understandable / and cry
down and up in a hole //

and spell the snow that just won't melt / on spring flowers and
monuments / on rubbish dumps and vases with ash //

the white silence gradually becomes greyer / and what the
words also want to unsilence /
the dead are dead, the page is black – //

HESTER KNIBBE

Anna responds to Tobit's accusation

Even blind you still think you're all-seeing, but / seeing you
were already blind. In my arms / I'm carrying what I earned
while you just grumble, make me / a scapegoat. With open
eyes //

you were asleep, now you're sitting there, the hem threadbare
/ on your robe, a mole, not worth kicking, you / the righteous
always generous, a miser / you've been, attached to power. No
//

Tobit, I'm no thief, you know that, / between our bleating
thankyou and please, for /
giving gives esteem, receiving makes nugatory, *that's* //

what bothers you. Rather wash your eyes / with the gall you
spit, scrub the haughty /
muck from your soul. And see! //

Yes

Love, yes there is always a body attached / and that makes it
and makes it, makes it //

awkward, sometimes. But it doesn't matter, we've already been
/ together so long now that we've stored ourselves / inside
each other, can't get lost can't go away any longer. //

Naturally, the premonitions creep under the skin, dance /
along when you dance, run along when you run, hang //

on the couch too, sitting there and later Falter / runs away
with your dreams, a winter plagues / the old river that wants
to flow. But it //

doesn't matter, and the sphinx / that sets us the riddle *who
who the most* is nothing /

to worry about, we'll just hold each other / by the hand, and
where the road ends we'll sleep. //

Back-wash

I

Never in picture frames, got cases / housed my little ones in
there. They were / too alive for strange eyes, too loud / for the

silence that was expected //

to surround me. I was early / to save them being bullied,
trampled, knocked / over. Because this much is certain, the
lion and lamb / no longer go together. I gave birth //

to irregularity after irregularity, inadmissible, a brief / gasp for
breath, while my breasts oversaturated, / no mother no mother
no, //

began to leak. Scared I longed / to cling on to necessity. //

*

But I couldn't get rid of them, that's why / I kept them in the
cases. //

Because it isn't something that you just / wear on the outside, a
T-shirt / trousers you get fed up of or wear out and //

it isn't something like nails / and hair that you cut off, what
you //

carried in you you don't want to lose. So that's the reason / for
the cases, a sort of a journey back to / another womb darkness.
What were they supposed to do //

with light in their eyes closed. //

(*The title 'Zog' means both breastmilk and back-wash*)

2

If I had been a marine animal with more than / seven tentacles, without thinking I would have / fanned the dust off them so that they //

could breathe. But I had to make do with only / one heart some brains and these two hands. //

I cherished fed nourished them with / thoughts of the future, but something inside them wouldn't / grow, crudely went wrong. Bathwater too //

hot or too cold, the wrong socks on? Hugged them / to death too little or too much, hair / cut too short, or put too tightly in braids? //

But even if they didn't want to, they must and would, I / cursed forced them to be happy while I knew / how life can sometimes. Slave work, forced labour. //

3

As big as he was, a giant child / he sat in a cart and didn't listen, had / strange wrong clothes on and the wind / picked up, but he didn't listen, //

pulled with an aged slow / hand an idiotically checked hoodie / over his blank astonishment, didn't see / his mother's panic //

who cried – there's a storm coming. He / just sat there far too unafraid, and too crudely / built for a cart: clay //

doll of almost two metres tall / that I breathlessly blew life into. //

4

Sleep just sleep in your chaos of silence / the trees will give you shade / and weave a gauze of coolness over you / and everything will hold its breath. //

mama the birds sing so soberly here / a black seasonless summer reigns / an overly-great scattering blossoms //

Your sunny smile is in the photo / your wonderful smile is in the photo. //

I sit in the coldness of stone. / The walls are meant to be white, but they're / breaking, other lives are seething / over there, through there. //

On my lap your marble body. / Don't keep your eyes so shut / I want to ask you, smile at your mother / get up, be a little lighter. //

No? / I will always carry you. //

ROB SCHOUTEN

On tour

One evening I iron a shirt / and go and hold a talk on a colleague. / My God, what language I come out with / about mysticism and travelling not to be there. / How good it is to see the ladies! //

And under the creaseless cotton / my skeleton holds me upright / in which the meal consumed / with the organiser slowly poo-ifies / in demi-sec piss from 1993. //

But it doesn't help. The poet is alone / in the landscape of the mind, / in spite of his tasty neighbour girls, / and he doesn't travel not to be there, / he travels for the travel expenses. //

The past

Long ago, though after the war / – Because I only know about that through word of moan – / That time which was then still called the present, / The following octet was able to occur. //

'The houses were chattering their teeth with their doors, / In each corner sat an appalling Moloch, / Tearing apart boys of my age / And a crooked monster was watching over my bed. //

I was sleeping in by chance, then Harpies came, / Each one to love me till I bled, / And in the morning, an enormous beaver rat was gnawing //

On everything that I had on my mind.' / Because I used the money from the collection / To feather my nest with poetry collections. //

During the week

Talking about authenticity, / there wasn't any interest for it today / and I myself lay in bed half fluey. / Only once was I called to the door / to take part in auto-da-fes, / To infect Witnesses of Jehova. //

Feeling nugatory I stayed in my robe / staring at the window urbi et orbi / without learning much about myself / or contemporaneous passers-by. / No, the future was nothing today. //

Meanwhile, it became evening, of course; / right over me someone was getting tastelessly fucked. / At 11, I said sleep well to no one / but false alarm, I lay awake till 4 o'clock / in knots of sheets and just sweating. //

I did finally fall asleep hating people, / Making myself emerge like a beaming god / into an airy, not too immense cosmos / that I also suddenly had to leave. / Not leaving anything behind there in haste / and in the morning my flu wasn't over. //

Disenchantment

Today I talked to someone in world views, / an old junk dealer who didn't offer much. / If you want to get rid of it it can't be much, / he said, and otherwise you ought to keep it. //

He encouraged me. Keep it, good friend, / what do you think you could get in exchange? / I don't have paradise with me for you / and between us, it isn't there. //

But I kept at it, stubborn and despairing. / What do you offer, I asked, sleep? madness? / women? mystical insight? maybe medicines? / Meaning? genius? maybe pity? //

Give it for nothing, he said – the wreck –, life / isn't obligatory,
dictate a suicide note, / I'll publish it for you for free / until you
interest everyone here. //

– There were people standing around us laughing. / I was their
pastime, they weren't mine. / Walk on, I cried, and go and
mourn me at home, / or swap with me, then I'll laugh at you.
– //

Forget your youth, the junk dealer calmly resumed, / don't
waste your time on absence /
or the cause and effect of something. / If there's a muse, go to
bed with her. //

– she doesn't want to, I said – all the better then, / one for the
ages, but move on from her / Begin again tomorrow and the
day after / don't worry about milky ways. //

Embittered I got home and drank very much / to sad music,
uninterrupted, / until I was dead drunk and continually
thought / that I'd made myself alone. //

Then without me it became daytime again / and I discerned
myself on my pillow, / without necessity but apparently
awakened / by something internal that I had to live with. //

I went onto the street and wasn't purified / nor did I suddenly
feel world news, / or nugatory in the full shopping streets / or
democratic or obliged to do anything //

The dealer was gone, I had a hangover / in a thousand and was
in search of nothing, / but didn't find it because there is little,
/ scarcely hope and also almost no loss. //

WILLEM VAN TOORN

In memoriam

I dreamt that you were lying beside me last night. / You were
already sick. You said: to my marrow / I belong to death. Do
you mind / that you can't come inside me? Hold me softly //

against you. I said: you were so white / and tired when I saw
you – and then invis- / ible in a coffin where I went off the
path, / into the rain and the village. Waiting grass //

lay beside the pit piled up in sods. / How are you here again.
You said: I still wanted / to do what I why had neglected to do:
/ talk with you in bed the way lives talk. / But what I am now
has no language with you. //

There was no lamp. So how did I see you. / I fell asleep in the
dream, you held me tight. / The room remained cold until far
in the day. //

from The reservoir

V

Now it's there, you see, night / and I are maybe only dreaming
that I'm asleep, / because I'm wide awake and ask / where he's
brought me. //

But he's no longer standing behind / me when I look around. I
am / alone in an empty street / of an endless suburb. //

It's not raining, but it seems / as if it ought to be: / the flats and city parks are as grey / as in a post-war film / that ends sadly. / What if he were, / my unknown comrade / to want to leave me behind / in an old world so still //

that I hear words in my own head / waking up? But then I suddenly see / where I am and what he's doing with me: / I've gone into a flat / and see in front of the grey window / my father in his chair. //

He recognises me again. I go and sit / next to him and take his hand. / behind the window is nothing, / as if the house is in a cloud. //

Did you see the horses, he smiles, / they cantered in the Lingewei / as if they were flying, the mist / had stolen their hooves, / and we hung on the manes, / boys, not afraid of anything. //

I say, that was the past, father, / almost a century ago. / How else would I know that / than from your stories. / But of you and me together, / what do you still know of that? //

That war of ours for example, / a human life long / never really over. 'Father, father, hanging / in our window is a burning beast, / look then, it's roaring straight at us.' / You carried me in your arms / Down flights of stairs and I was / almost no longer scared. That was / when you were strong and still far from dead / and I thought you must be a god. / Have I ever said that to you? //

And do you still know that music, / Haydn, that you most preferred / to play of all your records, / the string quartets? / He sees / the stranger that must be / his son. 'Did we have a gramophone then?' / he says, and his look streams empty. / He runs his hand across his eyes / and then the chair is deserted, / the window blurs and the room, / is irretrievably gone. //

Table
For Gerrit Kouwenaar

You think of a table for the poet, / lain in a limitless space, / on which mother time generously serves / the host that he always is / what he himself made edible of language: //

hills, fields and valleys, / in the depth the silvery strip / of river between blue vineyards / and the twisting path upwards, / to the house with the whispering rooms / that waits with the windows open. //

A comforting dis of earth, / and that the wind blows there, that light / falls there on grassy fields, / precisely in that one second / that the eye hits the mark fierce and unerring. //

You wish that an autumn garden / opens itself for him on command, / with lilies that raise themselves / like young ladies in the orchard, / and with grass that doesn't forget a footstep / that his hand writes into it. //

You want his table to remain so full. //

A crow near Siena

The way a crow flies over the hills near Siena: a crumpled black cloth above the / copper landscape. Working up a storm, you think from below, with those reverse wings. //

Through the binoculars its clever bill, its stubborn head: but he pulls it off. Not the / talented weaving of the swallows over the city – he remains an earthly //

sitter, who has thought: why can they damn it? And has risen to move / amazed to this much too great blue. //

The way these words move roughly from me to you. //

J. EIJKELBOOM

Afterwards

With difficulty I still know / that I could hate you terribly. / if I heard your knuckles crack /
on your too punctual journey / to bed, and how I fought / not to fall asleep myself / because what I didn't allow myself / was everything that you couldn't leave alone: //

the precise obligation, the strict belief. / Although I did bow my head too / before we ate our slice of bacon, / because I didn't want to hurt you. / But I couldn't talk to you any more, / I stranger, who loved you. //

Empty church

I

The tall carcass, the useless space, / pulpit and organ covered, an emptiness / that sucks the light into it. //

The boy who sat there on rock-hard, / now removed pews, once imagined / how you could swing from chandelier //

to chandelier like Tarzan and escape / the pastoral injunction
/ that stiffened the flock below him. //

What remained is an absence / that filled the whole space and
stretched / up to the barrel-vaulting, the crown of the skull //

of who stands here and undamaged / will later leave this
sanctuary. //

II

On the other hand the tombstones / have been laid outside
in the meantime, piled / like the bodies they once covered. //

The tombstones themselves were bared / when the plank floor
was lifted. / Yet, they are drastically worn, //

at least what there was of relief: arms, / festoons, as well as the
chubby cheeks / of cherubs, their once frisky genitals //

levelled out to a semi-colon; only / what was inscribed is still
readable / but no longer of importance. //

Sound

I

Meanings / are too numerous for words / but sink themselves
/ in seas of sound. //

The composer draws his tones out / but listens to much more.
/ Endlich fortissimo, cried Mahler / next to Niagara. //

But who understood that? / He that wrote it down / so that it continues to live: / the recorded word / and the spoken word / are not entirely superfluous – / that you will never / hear me say. //

II

John Cage stood in an echoless cell / and heard two sounds. /

The higher was his central nervous system, / the lower was his blood circulation. /

There is sound as long as you live, / and there'll be sound after you die. //

For music, Cage wrote in Silence, / there is therefore still all hope. //

Change of perspective

The view now brought back to this / end of a tiled roof, / a sky through the tangle / of a forgotten TV antenna. //

The high window to be reached if necessary / by ladder, but why? / It's as stuck as the wall / that it's contained in. //

But it lets light through from above / that could come out of eternity / if one believed in that. //

Sometimes it falls on a hand, a fist, / a wad in it that wanted to moan / but didn't get much further / than rustling. //

And then again it strikes a head / that looks up and sees: / there it's air-mail blue. //

It brings him someone to mind / who finely ground lavender / and then held her fingers / under his nose. //

Never before / was there such a modesty / of desire. //

Who writes history

– you walked beside me there / in your golden jacket. – / (21 November 1981) //

Is that jacket still lying somewhere, gold / that had already started wearing out then? / Through the cracks you saw moss-green leather. //

How differently I walked next to you / than when between other soldiers / I marched with my rifle. //

Other old servicemen / wrote in the air in the air then: / Just go and demonstrate in Moscow. //

Who writes history? / Not those who with their lightest steps / walk along in passionate parades. //

But also not the critical gentlemen / who from citadel or chamber / would think to dictate to a tidal wave. //

A day out of human sea? Or was it more? / A turnabout or new wine / for old poetry. I only know: //

We walked happily then, there, / in love with a hundred thousand people / and with each other too. //

1800

The hundred cities with gates locked at night. / In the canals,
churning with filth, the bacillus / cholera asiatica stirs. Moors
between the cities / dully flooding. Dry grounds watched over
by hunter and //

herder. On the eastern border around the villages are meadows:
/ fields with madder, flax, hop, hemp. Fens / have descended
into the water. Sometimes, in the streaks of mist, by / fireflies,
will-o'-the-wisps, as though hacked //

from an ice-hole, ivory, the oldest icon of the first face / drifts,
her throat ringed by pleated cloth over / the last wolf and
beaver. Her nose smells the scent //

of the waste land, lady-smock and sorrel. Soaking wet, / hard
and inhospitable his dark refuge / of grey villages; a cold little
people sits by wood smoke and fire. //

Shredding machines on the horizon

Sheep no longer: only the cunning wolf. / On the horizon,
shredding machines / unnoticeably chew what falls into them.
Inside / the aquarelles glitter; they are fish //

with bones and all pressed raw onto the stone. / Even the
Rhine is maybe a form of pain too /
like feet and voices, long forgotten / what drove them.
(Quartered mouths, half throats.) //

Swifter than evening wolves is the enemy / that hunts us: it is in a dead sea scroll / that this is still written. On a Stéle by Miró //

a round sun burns over what seems to be / a landscape, and with a river. As a constellation / what has to remain, in the world and us shines. //

The dust trail and the airplane magnet
  'I
quit'
Ahmad Shamlu

The dust trail with the dragon's head / that sways in the air current / never tires of repeating 'Dust / we are, only swaying dust' //

Only to the living does the airplane magnet / send its tiding / 'Always distrust the talking dust / and the sausage-grinder that grinds spirit' //

To the statues of dust particles: / 'Wheat fields, that is your lord / not every voice is a human's / in the carrion age of grinning ghosts' //

Cloned phantoms are dully rattling off / their echoes and mantras; fields / full of trooping threshers, and in the sea, / the muzzle of the cigar-shark is hastening //

In the lands of the blind, the cyclops / now keeps quiet, like Krakatoa / in the kingfisher time of Apollinaire, / the harbinger of the cold age //

Phantoms are calling down ruin because / phantoms want ruin and sleep / Outside the wind is blowing, children and / oh flocks of sheep, keep on the go //

Get out of the echo chambers

...Cancerous carnival of the flesh, / known as fairground of the body not soul / look in clear weather / a few sharply honed commas. //

...Viruses stamped in my forehead / like pitiful Samoyeds, / the back of my head on the other hand / ground with moronic dragoons. //

...My cap haven and harrying. / On the wall the whetstone. / Creaking carts, blind teamsters /
descended the Ore Mountain Ridge. //

Get out of my water catchment zones, / get out of the echo chambers; /
The heartbeat doesn't reside there, / there the hammer-blow pounds. //

Thieves emptied the clocks / and still the elder sprouts; / the blind in the quarters / strike up a new scream. //

Oh Hannover and stacked land! / Agricola left for Mainz, / bridges strike powder towers / and the accident ends. //

K. MICHEL

No and yes

No and yes is always there / more than one choice / and before you do something (or leave it) / you can always count to basta //

A quarrel needs two opinions / a kiss four lips / a body five litres of blood //

To make rain, a tree / a house, music, a dream / a number of elements are required //

And in the tracks of furtive animals / around a muddy drinking hole / countless stars glitter at night //

For someone who only thinks / with one (and not the other) / that number is a hammer / and the whole world is a nail //

Domino

There's a crack swimming through the house / Nobody that's listening //

Out of the shadows shadows grow / in the underwater light / that passing cars cast / on the walls around the bed //

In the deep-blue silence / a little boy repeats lip-softly / all that was said that day / and stitches word for word / the holes in the sound / that is called marriage //

The floor waves / The door-handle is far //

And the little boy holds the palms of his hands / like a book in
his hands / and I read 'come back, go away' //

A fairytale, a domino tile / that strikes a star / in the glass of
my house //

Then outside it begins / to snow bridal gowns //

Thumb-rules

If the residence is infested, they said / in the village of my
grandparents / then lock up a pig for a night long / the evil
will crawl into the animal / and the next morning everything
will be clean //

In the construction that each life is / a moment will arrive and
that's called / good advice was expensive, a leak / has covered
the walls with rorschach blots / and it smells of something
that was once / hidden during an old game //

Look around the table and try / to find out who the sucker
will be / thus goes a golden tip for poker players / if you don't
see the victim / then there's only one possibility left //

So I say this new day / to the face in the shaving mirror / stop
digging if you're in the hole /
be prepared to say ow & yes / look around you, search through
all rooms / and if you don't find the pig / then you're it //

It can be found on the inside

You think I'm pretty? I know the cold of mine / lying in shame in the extremely attentive breath of my maker. Never was I enough. //

That look of hers. Her hands that just kept on: / it isn't good, we'll put ears on, / melt little feet on, scour it with sand //

until it gleams, we'll scoop the sickness out / and burn it into form until it's something / that smoothly and elegantly can stand alone //

and painlessly keep silent, definitive, preferably in the shadow / of a room – whoever walks by and by chance / looks at it, must think: fine, that's what it's for. //

I am not this. I'm hidden in the place / where I was born as dung and straw / in the hollow under the mascara of my polished //

glass threads that to finally erase / the last wild strange unsightly remains of me, / she stuffed full with night-black. //

The fall

We crossed the Styx. / The ferryman lay drunk in his ship. / I held the rudder and we sank like stones. //

Water consists like the earth / of layers, transparent ribbons, gleaming strata / of ever smaller life, less warmth. //

Air bubbles bloomed in your hair, / the current pulled your head back / and stroked your throat. //

Stones waved with arms of algae and ferns, / sang softly gargling 'peace'. / They sliced your clothes loose. //

Fish licked blood from your legs. / I held your hand tight. I wanted to comfort you / but we were falling too fast and there are no words //

that exist without air, my love / stayed above, blue balloons, flares for a moment / marking the site of the accident //

before they drifted on. Your mouth opened. / Your face became red, your hands sought / balance, sought my arms. //

You tried to climb up inside me. / You were a glassblower with a cloud of diamonds / around his mouth. I held you tight as a kitten. //

I stroked your fingers. / You didn't let go. / You slept and I stroked your fingers, let go. //

WINDOWS
A note on the translations

A translator once told me that if he didn't understand a poem, he translated the words. While words are certainly the currency of these translations, versions and riff-offs, they do try to follow Pound's example of seeing the poem, or even poems, *through* the words. In contrast to musical notes, words don't have a universal pitch that can be waved through international border posts, and even notes trail the kite-tails of the cultures that arranged them.

There's an argument that our current conception of translation as the conveyance of meaning and style from one language to another may be more appropriate for prose, where semantic adherence to the narrative is the primary goal, and to a lesser extent drama, where compelling dialogue drives the play. But, increasingly, I have come to consider poetry translation as primarily a sensory mimetic activity.

There are three genera of poetry translator: the poet-occasionalist, the slavish-literalist, and, of course, the dedicated professional. Craig Raine's *Rashōmon*, an adaptation of Ryūnosuke Akutagawa's *In a Grove*, illustrates their respective taxonomies. In Raine's poem, a violation has taken place in a chance encounter on the Yamashina road, and somebody has to be brought to book for it, but there's some disparity in the witness testimony. The poet-occasionalist, sometimes unversed in the source language, is like Raine's samurai, swaggering 'bowlegged across the grove. His cock in its ruff of hair.' The poet-occasionalist is self-confident, appropriative, and although they will wish to commune with, or even possess the original, perhaps to make it an extra strand of their literary DNA, their conquest will merely be a straycation from a lawfully wedded oeuvre.

We see this clearly in the work of that serial straycationer Pound, where the focus lies on the artefact in English, not the original per se, which functions as engendering source material. Pound takes all the liberties necessary to deliver an English artefact in his Chinese versions and other translations. And if, by chance, he gets two poems mixed up, as he does when writing *The River Song* (which would be reputational suicide for a translator), we are more forgiving; it's Pound's creation that we're interested in, and his *interpretation* of Li Po, as much as Li Po himself. But, paradoxically, by taking liberties, modernising the diction, and focussing on the image, Pound more closely captures the spirit of the Chinese poetry than those late-Victorian poetasters with their superior understanding of the Chinese language. By putting his craft at Li Po's service, Pound pays him greater homage than the poetasters do, and he contributes something of value to our canon, indeed launches a literary movement, whereas the poetasters merely give us rumours of events elsewhere.

To return to *Rashōmon*, the slavish-literalist provides the inversion of the account of the violated wife. Here, we have a nineteen-year-old who's ostensibly been raped, and we instinctively sympathise with her, but her account doesn't ring true because of her exaggerations: 'I stabbed my throat and lived. I threw myself into a lake…I hanged myself and was rescued by my hands.' The tone jars with our experience. With the slavish-literalists, the reverse is the case. Our experience has taught us that poets are phrase-making originals, so when we are confronted with the syntactically awkward constructions of the slavish-literalist, we sense that the translation doesn't tally with the poetry, despite the literalist's inevitable appeal to the meaning of the source text. Because literal meaning is the fool's gold of poetry. Poetry is a multi-dimensional expression of a vision of reality through rhythm, sound, image and metaphor. If the translator fixates on the apparent literal meaning over the music, rhythm and tone, then they betray the poet, as we will find the wife did her husband in *Rashōmon*.

A poet chooses their words because of their sound taken in concert, and meaning and sound grow as an organic whole. I suspect that this is what Auden was suggesting when he commented that he didn't know what he thought until he wrote it down: meaning is partly generated and modified by the rhythm and music of the words. Here, Dylan Thomas's classification of poets who write *from* words and poets who write *towards* words is a tilting at windmills. Thomas is discussing eking coherence from a chaos of sound and image, but *all* poets write *from* words to varying degrees, depending on their aesthetic; but, translators always write *towards* words. While the poet is fumbling or striding towards a still nebulous end point, the translator's destination is cast perfectly on the wall of Plato's cave in the form of the original. However, if the source poet were to write in a different language, they would very likely choose other words than their literal transcriptions (and tellingly different from the translator's). They would choose the words that sounded the best to them, and meaning and even image – that one element of poetry that seems to transcend language – would quite possibly be modified by the opportunities offered in the new language. Therefore, understanding and anticipating a poet's style, tone and intention can give us some degree of latitude when sensorily mimicking their poems.

But, what of the professional translator, the source-shadower? Here, we can turn to Raine's murdered husband in *Rashōmon*, who must address the court through a medium. But, does the objective, dispassionate translator exist? I would suggest no and yes because the successful translator has to be a creative actor in their own right, simply because the source poem does not, and can never, exist beyond the language that it was written in. And so, the professional translator must construct an artifice. They shadow the original as closely as possible, while deviating enough to create a natural artefact in the target language. The extent of this deviation hinges on the writing talent and interpretive ability of the translator. This is the bread and butter of international literature, and though the translation is rarely the equal of the original, it is the reader's only window into the work of a foreign author.

And what does the foreign author want? To be translated as skilfully and carefully as possible, to have the artefact sound like literature in its own right, while remaining recognisably theirs. But two translations are never quite the same, as we will see from the two similar examples of Esther Jansma's *The Fall* below (and the more difficult the poem, the more divergent the translations will be):

> 'You tried to climb me. You were / a glassblower with a cloud of diamonds / at his mouth. I held you like a kitten. // I stroked your fingers. / You did not let go. / You slept and I stroked your fingers, let go. // (Francis R. Jones)

> 'You tried to climb up inside me. / You were a glassblower with a cloud of diamonds / circling his mouth. I hugged you like a kitten. // I stroked your fingers. / You held on tight. / You fell asleep. I stroked your fingers, let go. // (James Brockway)

Here, each translator gives us their own interpretation of the tone of the poem, using broadly similar words. They give us a close impression of what Jansma's poem will be like in Dutch; although Brockway lends his translation a dramatic tone because this is how he experiences the poem in Dutch. However, while both translations are successful, neither is as compelling as the original.

Another sub-genre of the professional translator that we have to consider is the translating poet, who knows the source language, such as Jamie McKendrick, Sasha Dugdale, George Szirtes, or Robert Minhinnick. The latter's *The Adulterer's Tongue* (translations of six Welsh poets) was the impetus for this collection. But, what distinguishes the translating poet from the translator: 1. Lower output; 2. Laborious years of working in the art-form itself; 3. The expectation that the finished artefact will be a poem in its own right and satisfy both the translating poet's ear and the original poet's. To demonstrate the influence of the translating poet, consider the second verse of Rilke's "Autumn Day":

> Command the last fruits to incarnadine; / vouchsafe, to urge them on into completeness, / yet two more south-like days; and that last sweetness, / inveigle it into the heavy vine. // (J.B. Leishman).

> Command the lingering fruits to ripen: / Grant them two southerly days yet / Then drive them to fulfilment and compel / The final sweetness in the heavy wine. // (Stephen Spender)

The translating poet attempts to inhabit rather than imitate the source poem, which is one reason that productivity can be low, sometimes amounting to a single volume, sometimes a single poem, but the work must be seen within the context of the poet's own oeuvre. But, what added value does the poet translator bring to international literature? Michael Hofmann pleads (in the case of Zbigniew Herbert and the Carpenters) for a single good, or preferably great, translator for a major poet. I would advocate against orthodoxy and for a plurality of voices to better appreciate a source poet. Reading multiple translations has rarely *reduced* appreciation or understanding of a poet, while one can certainly take issue with the hegemony of a single approved or authoritative translator. The ambition of the translating poet to create a stand-alone, multi-dimensional artefact must provide a sensorily satisfying experience of the source poem, as was intended by the original poet.

There is one final category in this collection to be considered: the riff-off. T.S. Eliot's *The Hippopotamus* being a case in point. Eliot transformed Gautier's witty original into a brilliant satire on the Roman Catholic church.

The hippopotamus and I
have an impenetrable hide.
In armour-plate of certainty
I roam the plains with dauntless stride.
(Gautier, translated by Timothy Adès)

Flesh and blood is weak and frail,
Susceptible to nervous shock;
While the True Church can never fail
For it is based upon a rock.
(T.S. Eliot)

This is the guiding principle for the riff-off: not to be derivative in the sense of the epigone, but to make an original contribution, making use of another text as a springboard. In a sense, Eliot and Gautier are co-authors: Eliot's poem could never have existed without Gautier's inspiration, and Gautier could never have written Eliot's *The Hippopotamus*. But the relationship is symbiotic, much like Christopher Logue's and Homer's, rather than exploitative like Shakespeare's and Holinshed's.

The concept of the window as frame for a perspective of reality is an overly familiar metaphor. The translator aspires to be a window on the work of the poet; the poet aspires to be a window on reality. But, crucially, the poet's window is selective and transformative: it makes visible only what strikes the imagination of the poet. After the poet is long gone, their house decayed, the window remains. This is what allows

Logue to sit at Homer's window and allude to phenomena that Homer never witnessed; for example, providing the film direction 'Cut to the fleet', or titling a section 'GBH', or having Prince Hector 'jive' upon his heel. Similarly, I have made use of Hans R. Vlek's window to re-visit a number of his poems since his death in 2016, such as *Headbangers* and *De Mortuis Nil Nisi Bonum*. Depending on one's perspective of Lao Tzu, one of us may have become the other's persona.

This collection is intended as an homage to the ten Dutch poets included. Robert Minhinnick wryly notes in *The Adulterer's Tongue* that the collection might contain a number of accidents and possible fatalities. A disclaimer that I'm sure will apply to *Grand Larcenies*.